Internet Linguistics

The Internet is now an integral part of contemporary life, and linguists are increasingly studying its influence on language. In this student-friendly guidebook, leading language authority Professor David Crystal follows on from his landmark bestseller *Language and the Internet* and presents the area as a new field: Internet linguistics.

In his engaging trademark style, Crystal addresses the online linguistic issues that affect us on a daily basis, incorporating real-life examples drawn from his own studies and personal involvement with Internet companies. He provides new linguistic analyses of Twitter, Internet security, and online advertising, explores the evolving multilingual character of the Internet, and offers illuminating observations about a wide range of online behaviour, from spam to exclamation marks.

Including many activities and suggestions for further research, this is the essential introduction to a critical new field for students of all levels of English language, linguistics and new media.

David Crystal is a freelance writer, lecturer and broadcaster, based in Holyhead, North Wales. He is author of numerous books including *Just a Phrase I'm Going Through* (Routledge 2009). The first Routledge David Crystal Lectures DVD, *The Future of Language*, was published in 2009.

'Crystal draws on his wealth of expertise to shed light on the important issues related to language form and use online.'

Mark Warschauer, *University of California, Irvine, USA*

'David Crystal is a master linguist and master teacher. Given his expertise on language and the internet, he is the ideal author for this student text.'

Naomi S. Baron, *American University, USA*

'Crystal provides a unique overview of authentic applications for linguistics on the internet and the methodological issues raised in the case-studies will be relevant for a wide range of projects that readers may be working on. This will become essential reading for students in this area.'

Charlotte Taylor, *University of Portsmouth, UK*

Internet Linguistics: A Student Guide

David Crystal

Routledge
Taylor & Francis Group

LONDON AND NEW YORK

First published 2011
by Routledge
2 Park Square, Milton Park, Abingdon, Oxon OX14 4RN

Simultaneously published in the USA and Canada
by Routledge
711 Third Avenue, New York, NY 10017 (8th Floor)

Routledge is an imprint of the Taylor & Francis Group, an informa business

© 2011 David Crystal

The right of David Crystal to be identified as author of this work has been asserted
by him in accordance with sections 77 and 78 of the Copyright, Designs and
Patents Act 1988.

Typeset in Sabon and Scala by
Swales & Willis Ltd, Exeter, Devon
Printed and bound in Great Britain by
TJ International Ltd, Padstow, Cornwall

British Library Cataloguing in Publication Data
A catalogue record for this book is available from the British Library

Library of Congress Cataloging in Publication Data
Crystal, David, 1941–
Internet linguistics : a student guide / David Crystal.
p. cm.
Includes index.
1. Computational linguistics. 2. Internet. 3. Internet—Social aspects. I. Title.
P98.5.I57C75 2011
004.601'4—dc22
2010034571

ISBN 13: 978-0-415-60268-6 (hbk)
ISBN 13: 978-0-415-60271-6 (pbk)
ISBN 13: 978-0-203-83090-1 (ebk)

CONTENTS

PREFACE

How does one write a student guide to a subject that does not exist – or, at least, does not yet exist in such a recognized form that it appears routinely as a course in university syllabuses or as a chapter in anthologies of linguistics? Inevitably, it will be something of a personal account, informed by the various Internet projects with which I have been involved. The situation reminds me of the 1980s, when pragmatics was evolving as a field of study, and the various published introductions differed widely in their subject-matter. Internet linguistics is at that inchoate stage now. I can easily imagine other introductions to the subject – written perhaps by someone with a background in computational linguistics – which would look very different from this one. My background is in descriptive linguistics, and it shows. But it is an appropriate background to have, for the one thing Internet language needs, more than anything else, is good descriptions.

A growing number of linguistics students, at undergraduate and postgraduate levels, are now beginning to study the subject, and I have written this book primarily for them. It will I hope also be of interest to those who are taking a language course as part of a degree in media or communication studies. I have assumed that readers have completed an introductory course in linguistics, or at least read an introduction to the subject, and are familiar with the various domains that constitute the Internet, including the most recent developments. They will not find here an exposition of syntax or sociolinguistics, or of blogging or social networking. It is an account written for people who are comfortable with the basic tenets and methods of linguistics, well versed in Internet activities, and curious about the relationship between the two. It is also for those, within this population, who are fascinated by the way Internet language is evolving, and want to research it. I have therefore given as many pointers as I could to topics where research is needed. My aim is not just to inform but to inspire more linguists to work in this field, for, as will become apparent – and surprising as it may seem – the subject is urgently in need of them. In particular, I have illustrated my points almost entirely from English, and this limitation needs to be overcome if the conclusions are to be robust.

This book is very different from my *Language and the Internet*. The emphasis in that work was on the stylistic diversity of the medium, so there was a focus on the linguistic features which identify language varieties. In the present book, general issues of characterization and methodology take centre stage. The descriptive chapter on Twitter would not have been out of place in the earlier book, but in other respects Internet linguistics tries to live up to its title and provide a wider perspective which *Language and the Internet* lacked. A certain amount of overlap has been inevitable, but I hope it is not intrusive.

My thanks are due to those who reviewed this text on behalf of the publisher, and also to Sacha Carton, Ian Saunders, and others in the companies (AND, Crystal Semantics, Adpepper Media) with whom I have had the opportunity to develop the approaches described in Chapter 6. Above all, I owe an enormous debt of gratitude to my wife and business partner Hilary, who has shared my close encounter with the Internet, professionally and privately, over the past 20 years.

David Crystal
July 2010

1

LINGUISTIC PERSPECTIVES

Wherever we find language, we find linguists. That is what linguists are for: to seek out, describe, and analyse manifestations of language everywhere. So when we encounter the largest database of language the world has ever seen, we would expect to find linguists exploring it, to see what is going on. It has begun to happen. And a new field is emerging as a consequence: Internet linguistics.

The name is not yet in universal use, partly because other terms have been proposed to focus on the communicative function of the Internet. In the 1990s, *computer-mediated communication* (CMC) became widely known, a usage which was much reinforced when it appeared in the title of an influential online publication, the *Journal of Computer-Mediated Communication*.[1] However, from a linguistic point of view, this term presented a problem: it was too broad. It included all forms of communication, such as music, photographs, line-drawings, and video, as well as language in the strict sense of the word. It is this 'strict sense' that forms the foundation of any course on linguistics, where linguists point out the important difference between spoken, written, and signed language, on the one hand, and such figurative notions as 'the language of painting' and 'the language of the face', on the other.[2] The terms *language* and *communication* are not synonymous.

The name *computer-mediated communication* is still widely used, though, as are two other terms which have an even broader remit. The emergence of mobile technology placed a certain strain on the notion of 'mediation by computer'. People do not really feel they are holding a computer up to their ear when they talk on their cellphone, notwithstanding the fact that a great deal of computational processing is involved in making the arrangement work. And the unease was increased by the proliferation of interactive speech devices. Whether a machine is talking to us (as with satellite-navigation car instructions or airport tannoy announcements) or we are talking to a machine (as with a telephone-booking service or a voice-activated washing-machine) or reading an e-book, we do not primarily think of the devices as 'computers'. Or, at least, they are very different 'computers' from the kind we are used to seeing on our desks or carrying in our briefcases. Many people have thus begun to use the more inclusive names *electronically mediated communication* (EMC) or *digitally mediated communication* (DMC). It is too soon to say which of these will become standard – or, indeed, whether some other name will emerge from cyberspace. Either way, from a linguistic point of view they are still too broad, blurring the distinction between language and other forms of communication.

I find *Internet linguistics* the most convenient name for the scientific study of all manifestations of language in the electronic medium. It provides the required focus, compared with human communication as a whole (for which the name *Internet semiotics* might be more appropriate). And it is certainly a more satisfactory label than some of those which were proposed in the early days of the Internet. *Cyberspeak*, *Netspeak*, and other *-speak* coinages were often used in accounts aimed at a general public,[3] but their weakness was that they placed undue emphasis on the potential linguistic idiosyncrasy of the medium and suggested that the medium was more homogeneous than it actually is. The predominance of English on the Internet led to such names as *Netlish* and *Weblish*, but *-lish* terms are far too restricting today, given the increased e-presence of Chinese and other languages.

Electronic discourse and *computer-mediated discourse* also had some use, and their focus on interaction and dialogue have kept them alive in a social networking era. The *e-* prefix generated *e-language* and *e-linguistics*, though neither seems to have caught on; nor has *cyberlinguistics*. Sometimes it was the kind of activity that generated a new label, as in the case of *searchlinguistics*. *Internet linguistics*, as I am using the term, includes them all, as does *netlinguistics*. It is the study of language on the Internet – or *language@internet*, as the title of an online journal has it.[4]

As a domain of academic enquiry, Internet linguistics is in its infancy, but we can see how it is likely to develop. All the recognized branches of linguistics are in principle available. We can anticipate studies of Internet syntax, morphology, means of transmission (phonological, graphological, multimedia), semantics, discourse, pragmatics, sociolinguistics, psycholinguistics, and so on. A balance needs to be maintained between the study of the formal properties of Internet language and the study of its communicative purposes and effects. As descriptive and theoretical findings accumulate, we can expect a fruitful domain of *applied Internet linguistics* to emerge, providing solutions to problems of language encountered by the various users of the Internet, such as in search, e-advertising, and online security. Indeed, as we shall see, a great deal of research into Internet language has already been motivated by applied considerations.

MISCONCEPTIONS

As has happened repeatedly in the history of language study, an important part of the linguist's job is to eliminate popular misconceptions, and the Internet has certainly provided plenty of these. The prophets of doom have been out in force, attributing every contemporary linguistic worry to the new technology, and predicting the disappearance of languages and a decline in spoken and written standards. When we investigate the worries, we invariably find they are based on myths. The moral panic that accompanied the arrival of text-messaging (or SMS, the 'short-messaging service') provides an illustration.

When text-messaging became popular in the UK, around the year 2000, many people saw it as a linguistic disaster. Five years later, when it began to be popular in the USA, the same reaction appeared there. There was a widespread belief that texting had evolved as a modern phenomenon, full of abbreviations that were being used in homework and exams by a young generation that had lost its sense of standards. A typical comment appeared in the *Daily Mail* in 2007 from the broadcaster John Humphrys. In an article headed 'I h8 txt msgs: How texting is wrecking our language' he says that texters are 'vandals who are doing to our language what Genghis Khan did to his neighbours eight hundred years ago. They are destroying it: pillaging our punctuation; savaging our sentences; raping our vocabulary. And they must be stopped.' He was not alone. Other disparaging comments have labelled the genre as 'textese', 'slanguage', and a 'digital virus'.

It was difficult to counter these views in the absence of relevant linguistic research. But several studies have now shown that the hysteria about the linguistic novelty (and thus the dangers) of text-messaging is misplaced. All the popular beliefs about texting are wrong. To summarize the results of a growing literature:[5] only a small part of text-messaging uses distinctive abbreviations (textisms); these abbreviations are not a modern phenomenon; they are not restricted to the young generation; young people do not pour them into their homework and exams; and texting helps rather than hinders literacy standards.

Text-messages are not 'full of abbreviations'. In one American study, less than 20 per cent of the text-messages showed abbreviated forms of any kind – about three per message. In a Norwegian study, the proportion was even lower, with just 6 per cent using abbreviations. In a collection I made myself, the figure was about 10 per cent. People evidently swallowed whole the stories that appear from time to time asserting that youngsters use nothing else but abbreviations when they text. The most famous case was a story widely reported in 2003 claiming that a teenager had written an essay so full of textisms that her teacher was totally unable to understand it. An extract was posted online, and quoted incessantly. The whole thing was a hoax – which everyone believed.

Nor are text-message abbreviations 'a modern phenomenon'. Many of them were being used in chatroom interactions that predated the arrival of mobile phones. Several can be found in pre-computer informal writing, dating back a hundred years or more. The most noticeable feature is the use of single letters, numerals, and symbols to represent words or parts of words, as with *b* 'be' and *2* 'to'. They are called rebuses, and they go back centuries. Adults who condemn a 'c u' in a young person's texting have forgotten that they once did the same thing themselves when they played word games. Similarly, the use of initial letters for whole words (*n* for 'no', *gf* for 'girlfriend', *cmb* 'call me back') is not at all new. People have been initializing common phrases for ages. *IOU* is recorded from 1618. There is no difference, apart from the medium of communication, between a modern kid's *lol* ('laughing out loud') and an earlier generation's *SWALK* ('sealed with a loving kiss').

Nor is the omission of letters – as in *msg* ('message') and *xlnt* ('excellent') – a new phenomenon. Eric Partridge published his *Dictionary of Abbreviations* in 1942. It contains dozens of SMS-looking examples, such as *agn* 'again', *mth* 'month', and *gd* 'good'. Texters also use deviant spellings, such as *wot* 'what' and *cos* 'because'. But they are by no means the first to use such nonstandard forms. Several of these are so much part of English literary tradition that they have been given entries in the *Oxford English Dictionary*. *Cos* is there from 1828 and *wot* from 1829.

The most important finding of the research studies is that texting does not erode children's ability to read and write. On the contrary, literacy improves. Strong positive links have been found between the use of textisms and the skills underlying success in standard English in pre-teenage children. Interestingly, the more they used abbreviations, the higher they scored on tests of reading and vocabulary. The children who were better at spelling and writing used the most textisms. And the younger they received their first phone, the higher their scores. Sample sizes are small, but the results all point in the same direction.

These results surprise some people. But why should we be surprised? Children could not be good at texting if they had not already developed considerable literacy awareness. Before you can write and play with abbreviated forms, you need to have a sense of how the sounds of your language relate to the letters. You need to know that there are such things as alternative spellings. You need to have a good visual memory and good motor skills. If you are aware that your texting behaviour is different, you must have already intuited that there is such a thing as a standard. If you are using such abbreviations as *lol* and *brb* ('be right back'), you must have developed a sensitivity to the communicative needs of your textees, because these forms show you are responding to them.

It will be a while before the moral panic surrounding the language of text-messaging dies down. It does not take long for a myth to be established in the mind of the general public, but it can take a lifetime to eradicate it. That is one of the chief responsibilities of linguists – to demythologize. They need to build up databases using larger samples, patiently publicize findings, and try to establish a more positive climate. They can also contribute to educational projects, suggesting ways in which the Internet in general (and text-messaging in particular) can be introduced into the classroom so as to facilitate learning about language. A fruitful exercise is the 'translation' of text-messages into a more formal kind of standard language, and vice versa, in order to develop the student's sense of the appropriateness of styles of language in particular situations. Several schools also engage in creative projects, such as the writing of text-messaging poetry.

What linguists cannot do is contribute professionally to the debates which take place about the social, psychological, legal, and other dangers associated with the Internet. Should a teacher confiscate a mobile phone being used by a student in class? Should parents control the amount of time their children spend on their computer? Should employers monitor the use of computers for work-unrelated activity? Should the Internet be censored? Should advertising be controlled? How can we prevent excessive keyboard or keypad use causing muscular damage? There are many such questions, about which I (as a human being) have my opinions; but these opinions do not relate to my expertise as a linguist. Rather, they fall under the remit of sociologists, psychologists, physiologists, educationalists, lawyers, and others. They are not part of an Internet linguistics, though applied linguistic collaborations with these other domains are likely to prove illuminating.

What I, as a linguist, see on the Internet is a remarkable expansion of the expressive options available in a language – far exceeding the kinds of stylistic expansion that took place with the arrival of printing and broadcasting. These earlier media introduced many new varieties of language, such as news articles, advertisements, sports commentaries, and weather forecasts. The same sort of thing has happened on the Internet, illustrated by such new varieties as email, chat, texting, blogging, tweeting, instant messaging, and social networking. The difference is that the Internet is so much larger than the earlier media – it is capable of subsuming the worlds of print and broadcasting – and changes more rapidly. We therefore need to learn to manage it, and this point applies not only to Internet content but also to the language in which the content is expressed.

It is not always easy to use language clearly and effectively on the Internet. The interaction between sender and receiver is different from traditional conversation. The anonymity of participants alters familiar communicative expectations. Written language on a screen does not behave in the same way as writing on a traditional page. We write it differently and we read it differently. It is easy to be ambiguous, misleading, or offensive, as is shown by the proliferation of netiquette guides which offer advice about how people should behave online. In short, we need to take care. But we cannot take care if we do not understand the strengths and weaknesses of the various linguistic options that are available to us. We need to understand how electronically mediated language works, how to exploit the strengths and avoid the dangers, and this is where the developing branch of Internet linguistics can make a significant contribution.

TERMINOLOGICAL CAUTION

Students of Internet linguistics need also to be aware that some of the terminology they associate with the subject of linguistic science appears on the Internet in a different guise. This is not the first time this has happened. Linguistics has often proved to be useful to other intellectual disciplines, which borrow its terms and then change their meaning. The Internet has done the same, notably with the words *semantic* and *semantics*.

Semantics began as a branch of linguistic science.[6] Indeed, the word *science* is used in its original definition: the French philologist Michel Bréal, who introduced the term in the 1890s, defined it as 'la science des significations' – the science of meaning in language. It came to be seen as a level of linguistic investigation, alongside phonetics, phonology, morphology, and syntax, in such seminal works as Leonard Bloomfield's *Language*; but the abstract and indeterminate nature of 'meaning' meant that it remained a neglected branch of linguistics for many decades. The first full-scale linguistic treatment was John Lyons' two-volume *Semantics* in 1977, now regarded as a classic statement of the 'state of the art' within linguistics and linguistic philosophy. In the meantime, in the absence of a linguistic characterization, other fields found the notion of semantics useful and began to employ it in individual ways.

The philosopher Charles Morris gave semantics a more general interpretation in 1946, defining it as the interpretation of signs in general – *signs* here being used in an abstract sense to include everything that conveys information. It therefore included facial expressions, bodily gestures, road signs, railway signals, and other non-linguistic systems. Also in the 1940s, the term achieved a certain notoriety in popular usage, where 'it's just semantics' began to refer to an irritating or pointless quibble. Psychologist Charles Osgood took the term in a different direction in 1953, referring to the judgements people make about words, and devising a system of rating scales which he called a 'semantic differential' – whether words are judged as strong/weak, good/bad, active/passive, and so on. Sometimes the term was narrowed, as when it began to appear in medicine with reference to a clinical syndrome – 'semantic aphasia', where people lose the ability to use words after brain damage. Sometimes it was broadened, as when Alfred Korzybski developed 'general semantics' in the 1930s as a method of enabling people to avoid the ideological traps built into language. But the term has achieved one of its widest extensions in the notion of the 'Semantic Web', where it includes all concepts and relationships within human knowledge.

'The vision I have for the Web is about anything being potentially connected with anything', says the web's inventor, Tim Berners-Lee, on the first page of his biographical account, *Weaving the Web*.[7] The Semantic Web will evolve 'without relying on English or any natural language for understanding', he says a little later. There could be no broader definition of semantics than that, and no definition that is further away from the original linguistic intention. The Semantic Web is seen to be an evolution of the web: the existing web is human readable, whereas the Semantic Web will be machine readable. Faced with the web in its current form, it is the human user who has to specify, find, and implement the links between one page or site and another; in the Semantic Web, the links will be processed by computers without human intervention. Both a linguistic and an encyclopedic dimension will be involved. For example, to achieve a presence for *automobile* on the Semantic Web, the linguistic definition (as found in a dictionary) would include such features as 'vehicle', 'wheels', 'drive', and 'road'; the encyclopedic account would include such elements as the different makes of car, their cost, and their safety record.

Semantics has achieved a buzz word status on the Internet these days, with many companies and approaches to knowledge management calling themselves 'semantic' (see further, Chapter 6). It must not be assumed that they are all talking about the same thing, or focusing on the same aspects of language. And this cautionary note applies in principle to any use of a linguistic term when found in the context of the Internet.

A rather different terminological question is what to call the various entities which form Internet discourse, such as email, blogs, chats, and tweets. A main aim of Internet linguistics is to establish their linguistic character. They are often described as *genres*, but that suggests a homogeneity which has not yet been established. The same question-begging would arise if they were called *varieties* or *dialects* or *registers* or any of the other terms for situationally related uses of language provided by sociolinguistics and stylistics. Linguists have to demonstrate linguistic coherence, not assume it. We need a term that is theoretically neutral, from the linguistic point of view, and for the present book I propose to use *outputs*. I shall talk about email, for example, as being one of the outputs of Internet technology. The term implies nothing about its linguistic character, or how it relates to other outputs.

RESEARCH CHALLENGES

There are several properties of Internet language which constitute a challenge to linguists wanting to explore this medium. The amount of data it contains, first of all. There has never been a language corpus as large as this one. It now contains more written language than all the libraries in the world combined, and its informational content is rapidly increasing as more parts of the world come online, video storage grows (via such networks as YouTube), and voice-over-Internet becomes routine.

Secondly, there is the diversity of the language encountered on the Internet. The stylistic range has to recognize not only web pages, but also the vast amount of material found in email, chatrooms, virtual worlds, blogging, instant messaging, texting, tweeting, and other outputs, as well as the increasing amount of linguistic communication in social networking forums (over 170 in 2011) such as Facebook, MySpace, Hi5, and Bebo. Each of these outputs presents different communicative perspectives, properties, strategies, and expectations. It is difficult to find linguistic generalizations that apply comfortably to Internet language as a whole.

Part of the reason for this is another linguistically challenging property: the speed of change. It is not easy to keep pace with the communicative opportunities offered by new technologies, let alone to explore them in the required linguistic detail. By way of anecdotal illustration, the first edition of my *Language and the Internet* appeared in 2001: it made no reference to blogging and instant messaging, which had achieved little public presence at that time. A new edition of the book was therefore quickly needed, and that appeared in 2006. It included sections on the language of blogs and of instant messages, but it made no reference to the social networking sites, which had achieved little prominence, and certainly no mention of Twitter, which arrived in the same year. Linguistic studies of the Internet always run the risk of being out of date as soon as they are written.

Even within a single output, it is difficult to keep pace. How can we generalize about the linguistic style of emails? When email first became prevalent, in the mid-1990s, the average age of emailers was in the 20s. Today, it is in the late 30s: the average in the UK rose from 35.7 to 37.9 in the year October 2006 to October 2007, according to Nielsen Online.[8] Doubtless similar increases are to be found in other countries. This means that many emailers, for example, are now senior citizens – 'silver surfers', as they are sometimes called. The consequence is that the original colloquial and radical style of emails (with their deviant spelling, punctuation, and capitalization) has been supplemented by more conservative and formal styles, as older people introduce their norms derived from the standard language.

Another example of rapid change comes from Twitter, which uses a prompt to elicit a user response. In November 2009 the nature of the prompt changed from 'What are you doing?' to 'What's happening?' As the Twitter blog explained:

> The fundamentally open model of Twitter created a new kind of information network and it has long outgrown the concept of personal status updates. Twitter helps you share and discover what's happening now among all the things, people, and events you care about. 'What are you doing?' isn't the right question anymore – starting today, we've shortened it by two characters. Twitter now asks, 'What's happening?'[9]

The blogger added: 'We don't expect this to change how anyone uses Twitter'. But in fact a change from an inward-looking question to an outward-looking one could not fail to alter the content of the site. Twitter now has far fewer isolated postings and far more semantic threads (see further, Chapter 3). In the terminology of classical linguistics, we are faced with a new language state (Saussure's *état de langue*), which raises the question of how we investigate the old ones.

For most people, the Internet became a reality following the arrival of the web in 1991, and a searchable reality after the arrival of Google in 1999. In that time, it went through several changes, reflecting the technological developments of the time. Each of these changes will have had linguistic consequences. For example, the kinds of constraint which gave a particular linguistic character to online games (MUDs, MOOs) in the 1990s have long been superseded. This means that the language of those games (1990s era) is in some ways like a period in the history of a language, needing to be studied in its own terms. But defining the boundaries of that period proves to be extremely difficult. The start-point of a new language output is relatively easy to establish, as it is linked to the innovative technology: people conversant with the history of the science can say with some precision when the language we associate with text-messaging, blogging, and tweeting began. What is more difficult is to identify endpoints, when a technology becomes outmoded or evolves into something different. And even when one has a sense of start- and end-points, tracking down the relevant data can be surprisingly difficult.

The Internet is sometimes wonderfully specific about its temporal identity, and at other times frustratingly inspecific. Beneath every page there is information about when the page was created; but only in a proportion of instances does that date appear on screen. This can cause great confusion, when (for example) a search for the population of a country yields several conflicting figures, and it remains unclear whether these reflect a synchronic or a diachronic perspective. When dates do appear, they are sometimes incomplete: many news sites, for example, give the day and the month, but not the year. There are techniques for finding the creation date of a page, or the date when the page was first spidered by a search engine or later updated, but they are cumbersome to nonspecialists.

When the dates *are* available, linguists find themselves faced with a different kind of problem: how to handle the unprecedented specificity? Linguists are used to being vague when it comes to describing language change: a word is said to have entered the language 'in the early sixteenth century' or in 'the

1780s'. Indeed, with rare exceptions, it has been impossible to identify the precise moment at which a new word or sense arrives in a language. But the time-stamping of web pages, and the ability to track changes, opens up a whole new set of opportunities. If I introduce a new word such as *digitextualization* on my website tomorrow at 09.42, it will be possible for lexicographers to say that the first recorded use of this word was at 09.42 on that day. This sort of chronological specificity has hitherto been of professional interest only to forensic linguists, concerned to identify patterns of criminal interaction, but it will in future be of much broader relevance. It is not yet clear how Internet linguistics will handle this level of descriptive detail.

Finally, leaving aside questions of dating, some kinds of Internet language present a rather different kind of challenge: inaccessibility. There is of course no problem in finding and downloading data from the pages of the web, within the various legal and commercial constraints imposed by website-owners. But it is a different matter when dealing with such outputs as email, chat, and text-messages. People are notoriously reluctant to allow their private e-communications to be accessed by passing linguists. There are now some excellent corpora of emails and chatroom interaction, but issues of reliability and representativeness have yet to be fully explored, and some domains, such as text-messaging, remain elusive, especially in languages other than English. The research literature is characterized by a great deal of theoretical speculation but relatively few empirical studies.

Another research issue arises out of the practice of anonymity. Normally, linguists take great pains to establish the situational factors which motivate or condition a use of language. Factors such as age, gender, class, and ethnicity are critical. But in a medium where a large number of participants hide their identity, or where we cannot trust the self-disclosed information about themselves which they place online, it is difficult to know how to interpret observed usage. Even fundamental distinctions, such as whether a netizen is male or female, or a native or non-native speaker, can be obscured. The Internet is not the first medium to allow interaction between individuals who wish to remain anonymous, of course, as we know from the history of telephone and amateur radio; but it is certainly unprecedented in the scale and range of situations in which people can hide their identity, especially in chatgroups, blogging, and social networking. The effect of anonymity on linguistic behaviour also needs to be explored. Operating behind a false persona seems to make people less inhibited: they may feel emboldened to talk more and in different ways from their real-world linguistic repertoire. They must also expect to receive messages from others who are likewise less inhibited, and be prepared for negative outcomes. There are obviously inherent risks in talking to someone we do not know, and instances of harassment, insulting or aggressive language, and subterfuge are commonplace.

Ethical considerations also need to be taken into account: what kinds of permission are needed to use Internet data? The same questions that linguists had to address in the 1960s, in the early days of corpus construction – such as the distinction between public and private language – have risen again in electronic form. If I send a message to the Internet, I have presumably let it go into the public domain: do I then have any right to object if a linguist includes it in a corpus? Who owns the text-messages in my mobile phone archive: are they mine or the senders'? In an increasingly litigious world, linguists need to take care that their data-collection procedures are robust with respect to the question of ownership.

As the old saying goes: turn a challenge over and you see an opportunity. The Internet offers linguists unprecedented opportunities for original research. Because we are dealing with an electronic medium, we need to not only investigate the new kinds of language introduced by the technology (blogging, tweeting, etc.), but also reinterpret everything we already know about language as realized through the older mediums of speech, writing, and sign. Whatever facts were established about, say, the differences between spoken and written vocabulary and grammar, these now have to be revisited, because the way we use language on the Internet is different in salient respects from the way we use it in traditional speech and writing. Which Internet styles of writing promote the use of abbreviations and emoticons? How does column width affect discourse structure? Do hypertext links influence the way a written text is organized? How does speech lag affect the character of a spoken conversation on Skype or iChat? Every use of language on the Internet will display features that do not correspond to the features identifying that use in traditional speech or writing. Written language has to be graphically translated[10] so that its content appears clearly on screen and can be easily accessed and navigated. Spoken language too needs to be processed so that its content can be indexed and navigated, with the possibilities here dependent on progress in automatic speech recognition.

Even when the electronic medium simply scans texts for viewing on screen, it presents those texts in new ways, allowing us to do new things with them. We can zoom in on an ancient manuscript and see detail that was not easily visible before, or carry out linguistic searches which were not practicable before. Well-studied uses of speech and writing appear in fresh guises. News journalism, for example, can look very different on screen compared with how it would appear in the traditional medium of print – paragraph size, for example, is often shorter. A poem on a screen is a very different reading experience from one in a printed book, especially when, as in text-messaging poetry, the small screen allows only a small part of the poem to be seen at any one time. The novelty is most apparent in the written language, for the Internet to date has been a predominantly graphic medium; but spoken language is also affected. Even the 'listen again' feature in a broadcasting station offers new possibilities: the programme is the same as it was on the radio, but the listener now has the opportunity to stop it at will, to listen to something a second time, to skip sections, and to move forwards and backwards along the timeline. The management of the auditory experience has transferred from the producer to the receiver.

The first step, then, in an Internet linguistics, is to establish the properties of the medium which condition the language experience and behaviour of its users. The most illuminating way of doing this, in my view, is to start by distinguishing it from the familiar worlds of spoken and written language.

See also 'Research directions and activities', p. 151.

2

THE INTERNET AS A MEDIUM

Linguists have been used to thinking of language in terms of speech and writing ever since the subject began. In due course, signing was added to make it a triad. When these dimensions are defined, great reliance is placed on the notion of *medium* (or *modality*, in some studies) – for speech, the phonic medium (air); for writing, the graphic medium (marks on a surface); for signing, the visual medium (hand movement and facial expression). Now we have a fourth dimension of linguistic communication – an electronic or digital medium.

How are we to compare mediums of communication? The anthropological and zoological approaches to semiotics have shown us the fruitfulness of a design-feature framework, in which salient properties of communication are identified and used as a basis of comparison. In linguistics, this procedure was first introduced by Charles Hockett in his comparison of language with animal communication.[1] The approach essentially asked the question: what does Medium A do that Medium B does not do, and vice versa? Language, for example, displays the property of displacement (the ability to talk about events remote in space or time from the situation of the speaker), whereas gibbon calls, for example, do not (the cries reflect immediate environmental stimuli). Hockett's approach brought to light an important point: that not all animal communication is the same. In relation to displacement, for example, bee dancing shares some properties with human language.

We can apply this approach to the Internet. The aim is to establish whether the electronic medium makes Internet language different from that found in other mediums, and, if we encounter differences, to examine why they are there. In view of the technological range and speed of development of the Internet (as summarized in Chapter 1), we must not expect the answers to be the same for all outputs. The relationship of the language to its associated technology will vary. The situations in which the language is used will vary. But we will expect to find certain common properties, or at least parameters in terms of which different outputs can be measured.

How are we to establish these properties? A first approximation can be obtained by comparing the Internet with spoken and written language. It has often been pointed out that the way we talk about the Internet suggests an uncertainty over the relationship with these two mediums. On the one hand we talk about having an email 'conversation', entering a 'chat' room, and 'tweeting'. On the other hand we talk about 'writing' emails, 'reading' web 'pages', and sending 'texts'. Is Internet language closer to speech or to writing, or is it something entirely different?

SPEECH VS WRITING

After half a century of research in several general and applied linguistic domains, such as grammar, lexicography, stylistics, and foreign language teaching, the chief differences between speech and writing have been clearly identified.[2]

Speech is time bound, dynamic, and transient; it is part of an interaction in which both participants are usually present, and the speaker has a particular addressee (or several addressees) in mind. Writing is space bound, static, and permanent; it is the result of a situation in which the writer is usually distant from the reader, and often does not know who the reader is going to be.

With speech there is no time lag between production and reception, unless one is deliberately introduced by the recipient. The spontaneity and speed of most speech exchanges make it difficult to engage in complex advance planning. The pressure to think while talking promotes looser construction, repetition, rephrasing, and comment clauses (such as *you know*, *you see*, *mind you*). Intonation and pause divide long utterances into manageable chunks, but sentence boundaries are often unclear. By contrast, with writing there is always a time lag between production and reception. Writers must anticipate the effects of this lag, as well as the problems posed by having their language read and interpreted by many recipients in diverse settings. Writing allows repeated reading and close analysis, and promotes the development of careful organization and compact expression, with often intricate sentence structure. Units of discourse (sentences, paragraphs) are usually easy to identify through punctuation and layout.

With speech, because participants are usually face to face, they can rely on such extralinguistic cues as facial expression and gesture to aid meaning (feedback). The lexicon is often vague, using words which refer directly to the situation (deictic expressions, such as *that one*, *in here*, *right now*). With writing, lack of visual contact means that participants cannot rely on context to make their meaning clear; nor is there any immediate feedback. Most writing therefore avoids the use of deictic expressions, which are likely to be ambiguous.

Many words and constructions are characteristic of (especially informal) speech, such as contracted forms (*isn't*). Lengthy coordinate sentences are normal, and are often of considerable complexity. There is nonsense vocabulary (e.g. *thingamajig*), obscenity, and slang, some of which may appear as graphic euphemism (*f****). Writing displays different characteristics, such as multiple instances of subordination in the same sentence, elaborately balanced syntactic patterns, and the long (often multi-page) sentences found in some legal documents. Certain items of vocabulary are never spoken, such as the longer names of chemical compounds.

Speech is very suited to social or 'phatic' functions, such as passing the time of day, or any situation where casual and unplanned discourse is desirable. It is also good at expressing social relationships and personal attitudes, due to the vast range of nuances which can be expressed by the prosody and accompanying nonverbal features. Writing is very suited to the recording of facts and the communication of ideas, and to tasks of memory and learning. Written records are easier to keep and scan, tables demonstrate relationships between things, notes and lists provide mnemonics, and text can be read at speeds which suit a person's ability to learn.

With speech, there is an opportunity to rethink an utterance while the other person is listening (starting again, adding a qualification). However, errors, once spoken, cannot be withdrawn; the speaker must live with the consequences. Interruptions and overlapping speech are normal and highly audible. With writing, errors and other perceived inadequacies can be eliminated in later drafts without the reader ever knowing they were there. Interruptions, if they have occurred while writing, are also invisible in the final product.

Unique features of speech include most of the prosody. The many nuances of intonation, as well as contrasts of loudness, tempo, rhythm, pause, and other tones of voice, cannot be written down with much efficiency. Unique features of writing include pages, lines, capitalization, spatial organization, and several aspects of punctuation. Only a very few graphic conventions relate to prosody, such as question marks and italics. Several kinds of writing (e.g. timetables, graphs) cannot be read aloud efficiently, but have to be assimilated visually.

When speech and writing are analysed in this way, it is plain that it would be simplistic to treat them as two self-contained and homogeneous entities. Varieties of language can be shown to combine some of the above characteristics in different degrees. It is more realistic to think of speech and writing as being the end-points of a multidimensional continuum, within which varieties can be located as being 'more or less like speech' and 'more or less like writing'. The varieties that form the Internet can be approached in the same way.

THE INTERNET AS A MIXED MEDIUM

Internet language outputs vary with respect to their similarities with speech and writing. At one extreme is the web, which in many of its functions (such as reference publishing and advertising) is no different from traditional situations that use writing; indeed, many varieties of written language (science, law, journalism, etc.) can now be found on the web with little stylistic change – none at all, if an exact digital copy has been made. In contrast, email, chat, instant messaging, and texting, though expressed through the medium of writing, display several of the core properties of speech. They are time governed, expecting or demanding an immediate response; they are transient, in the sense that messages may be immediately deleted (as in emails) or be lost to attention as they scroll off the screen (as in chatgroups); and their utterances display much of the urgency and energetic force which is characteristic of face-to-face conversation.

In relation to speech, the visual interaction of such packages as Skype and iChat, or the split screens used in some kinds of textual chat, is the closest we get to face-to-face interaction, though the ever-present lag between message transmission and reception denies it the simultaneity we encounter in everyday conversation. When the visual dimension is absent, instant messaging can approximate to the dynamic give and take of a conversation, though lacking the property of simultaneous feedback (see below). In chatgroups, the pressure on individuals to respond is still there, but less strong because the responsibility is shared. With social networking forums and Twitter conversations, there is no obligatory time-based dynamic, though many participants do respond to incoming messages promptly. With email, there is greater flexibility over delaying a response. With blogging and most web pages, responses are optional, even when solicited.

The outputs vary greatly with respect to their linguistic idiosyncrasy and complexity. At one extreme we find the web, which displays the same range of written constructions and graphic options as would be found in the corresponding texts of traditional print. Online government reports, newspaper editions, or literary archives (such as Project Gutenberg) have a great deal in common with their offline equivalents (though there is never identity, as screen and page offer different functionalities and constraints). At the other extreme, the character limits of texting and tweeting reduce the grammatical and graphic options, and the more elaborate sentence patterns do not appear. In between, we find outputs, such as blogging, that vary greatly in their constructional and graphic complexity. Some blogs are highly crafted; others are wildly erratic, when compared with the norms of the standard written language. Emails vary enormously: some people are happy to send messages with no revision at all, not caring if typing errors, spelling mistakes, and other anomalies are included in their messages; others take as many pains to revise their messages as they would in non-electronically mediated communication settings.

Internet outputs also vary greatly with respect to their communicative functions. There is a great deal of factual content on the web, and in blogs and emails. Chatrooms and social networking sites are highly variable: the more academic and professional they are, the more likely they are to be factual in aim; the more social they are, the more likely they are to contain sequences which have negligible factual content. Instant message exchanges are also highly variable, sometimes containing a great deal of information, sometimes being wholly devoted to social chit-chat.

On the whole, Internet language is better seen as writing which has been pulled some way in the direction of speech rather than as speech which has been written down. However, expressing the question in terms of the traditional dichotomy is misleading. Internet language is identical to neither speech nor writing, but selectively and adaptively displays properties of both. It is more than an aggregate of spoken and written features. It does things that neither of the other mediums does.

DIFFERENCES WITH SPEECH

Simultaneous feedback

The most important difference is the lack of simultaneous feedback. In a conversation, listeners perform an active role, using vocalizations (such as *mhm* and *really?*), facial movement (such as nodding and laughing), and gestures (such as hand movements and shrugging) as a running commentary on the interaction. Speakers unconsciously take note of this feedback and modify their speech accordingly. The feedback acts as an index of 'how we are doing'. If we say something ambiguous or potentially offensive, it can be queried straight away. If we are uncertain of how to put something, we can check with our listeners.

In Internet situations, simultaneous feedback is invariably absent. When someone is writing an email, there can be no such feedback, because the recipient is unaware of the impending message. Successive feedback will arrive, but not simultaneous. Even in so-called 'instant' messaging, while the fragment of dialogue is being typed there is no simultaneous feedback. And even in an apparently face-to-face situation, such as two people sending messages to a split screen at the same time, or a dialogue using visual Skype, there is a lag which can cause conversational interference, making the participants unsure about the relationship between turns. In an audio situation, people find themselves talking at the same time and having to repeat what they said when it becomes apparent that the other person has not heard them. Things will improve as the technology matures, but Internet conversations currently lack the kind of immediate mutual responsiveness that we take for granted in everyday dialogue.

Linguists need to explore the consequences of this. If users of the Internet cannot rely on obtaining simultaneous feedback from their interlocutors, what effect does this have on the way they use language? To take one example: an important feature of informal conversation is its use of reaction signals, comment clauses, and tag questions (such as *mhm*, *you know* and *isn't it?*), which give the listener the option of providing feedback. In a situation where this feedback is missing, will such features continue to be used, or will they be adapted in some way? My impression is that they are generally absent, but we need descriptive studies. And if they are absent, we need to analyse what the effect of this will be. Some writers have suggested that the lack of these features is one of the reasons why so many Internet interactions are misperceived as abrupt, cold, distant, or antagonistic. Addressing someone on the Internet is a bit like having a telephone conversation in which a listener is giving us no reactions at all: it is an uncomfortable and unnatural situation, and in the absence of such feedback our own language becomes more awkward than it might otherwise be.

Are people aware, when writing an email, that their language is autonomous – that they are 'on their own'? Judging by the comments of neophyte emailers, the answer is no. Most of us can recall cases where we sent an email, received an unexpectedly upset reply, and on rereading our message realized we had said something we had not intended to say. People doubtless learn from their mistakes. Netiquette guides repeatedly advise that we read emails through before sending them, and similar advice is relevant for all social networking situations. But the guides are notably unhelpful when it comes to giving specific advice about those aspects of grammar, vocabulary, orthography, and style which will help or hinder the efficacy of an Internet exchange. Most simply adopt old prescriptive attitudes, repeating artificial grammatical shibboleths such as avoiding the passive voice. We need more sophisticated, linguistically informed accounts of why some Internet exchanges are more successful than others.

Emoticons

It was an early awareness of the dangers of ambiguity which led to the development of emoticons. Apart from in video interactions, Internet exchanges lack the facial expressions, gestures, and conventions of body posture and distance (the *kinesics* and *proxemics*, as they are called in semiotics) which are so critical in expressing personal opinions and attitudes, and in moderating social relationships. The new symbols, such as the basic pairing of :) and :(for positive and negative reactions respectively, were intended to remove attitudinal ambiguity. Today there are over 60 emoticons usually offered by message exchange systems, and some dictionaries list several hundred possibilities using orthographic features (such as constructing ~(_8^(|) to identify Homer Simpson). However, despite the creative artistry, the semantic role of emoticons has proved to be very limited. An individual emoticon can still allow many readings – the basic smile, :), for example, can mean sympathy, delight, amusement, and much more – and these can be disambiguated only by referring to the verbal context. Without care, moreover, they can increase misunderstanding: adding a smile to an utterance which is ironic can be taken negatively as well as positively.

Usage is therefore changing. Emoticons were never very frequently used – one study showed only 13 per cent of emails contained them[3] – and they seemed to be used more by young people. Some linguists have interpreted this to mean that adults have better communicative skills: they do not need to rely on the crude attitudinal approximations that emoticons provide. On the other hand, adults are quite prepared to use an emoticon to replace an entire utterance – an emoticon with a broad grin, for example – in a situation where speed of response is at a premium, such as an instant messaging exchange. A lot depends on the output: an utterance consisting solely of an emoticon would be unusual in Twitter, where there is an expectation that messages should be to some degree semantically self-contained. There are also sociolinguistic and stylistic factors constraining our use of these symbols. Is it the case that the more serious the content, the fewer the emoticons? Or the more formal the interaction, the fewer the emoticons? Is there a correlation between emoticon use and age, gender, or ethnicity? In one instant messaging study,[4] three-quarters of the 16 females used emoticons, but only 1 (in 6) of the males. We need more studies of who uses emoticons, when, where, and why, in each kind of Internet activity.

Multiple conversations

In a traditional speech setting, it is impossible to hold a conversation with more than one or two people at a time. Entering a room in which several conversations are taking place simultaneously, we cannot pay attention to all of them or interact with all of them. But in real-time multi-party settings on the Internet, this is perfectly feasible and normal. In a chatroom, for example, we observe messages from other participants scrolling down the screen: there may be several conversations going on, on different topics, and we can attend to them all, and respond to them, depending only on our interest, motivation, and ability to type. It is not clear how people communicate effectively, under such circumstances. Short sentences, abbreviated words, punctuation avoidance, and other strategies motivated by economy account for some of the stylistic features of chat, but complex sentences can be encountered, and there is a great deal of individual variation.

Nor is it clear how participants cope with the vagaries of turn-taking, when several people are involved, and when the order in which messages (transmission units) appear on a screen is dependent on factors that are beyond the control of the participants. Messages are posted to a screen linearly, in the order in which they are received by the system. In a multi-user environment, they are coming in from various sources all the time, and with different lags, because of the way packets of information are sent electronically through different global routes. A reaction to a particular stimulus (such as a response to a question) can be separated by an unpredictable number of other utterances. Even in a two-way interaction, such as an instant messaging exchange, the usual linear organization of face-to-face conversation can be disrupted by a range of factors. Participant N may briefly leave the interaction, while Participant P, unaware of N's absence, continues to send messages. N then returns and 'catches up' in a string of responses to P. If P has made three points (let us call them 1, 2, and 3), then N's responses to each point (1r, 2r, and 3r) will be seen as a block, so that on screen what we see is 1, 2, 3, 1r, 2r, 3r, and not (as in an offline conversation) 1, 1r, 2, 2r, 3, 3r. Such a situation is bound to have some effect on the way the discourse grammar operates. Are responses governed by the same rules of ellipsis as are found in face-to-face conversation? What constraints might there be on the use of anaphoric pronouns? Could sequence of tenses be affected? There are many such questions awaiting investigation.

A basic question is: how often does this happen? In two-way (dyadic) interactions, the figure seems to be quite low. In a Swedish study of over 1,500 dyadic instant messaging utterances, only 10 per cent of the utterances were not adjacent to the utterance to which they related.[5] In data of my own, the corresponding figure was 15 per cent, but with considerable variation across conversations (from 4 per cent to 27 per cent). Even so, we are not talking large numbers: the majority of utterances respect adjacency. In the cases that do not, several factors seem to be involved. The subject-matter of the conversation is one, as a discussion of a serious topic to which both parties are contributing will motivate more sequences of utterances on each side, and there will be more 'talking at the same time', with specific points interacting in various ways. Overlapping is also likely to occur at the point where one party introduces a change of topic, as in utterance (U) 19 below:

15 H had you been to Steve's house before?
16 L no,
17 L is cute
18 H isn't it
19 H i'm working at home today
20 H the alarm man's coming to reset the alarm
21 L bit scary with a 2 yr old – lots of light colours!
22 L ok, me too . . .
23 H isn't it!
24 L dad too?

U21 continues the topic of U15–18, U22 responds to U19, U23 responds to U21, and U24 takes further U19. This is partly a function of the time lag between utterances. If H had waited longer before sending U19 and U20, L's U21 would probably have continued the theme of Steve's house in the appropriate place, and U22 would have followed U19. Instant messaging logs are only a partial reflection of the discourse realities. The lag makes them appear to be more incoherent than in fact they are.

It might be thought that disruption to turn-taking would inevitably lead to a breakdown in communication, but analysis suggests that this is not so. In the Swedish study referred to above, of the 144 utterances coded as relating to a non-adjacent previous utterance, 126 (87.5 per cent) caused no misunderstanding. In my family data, there was no misunderstanding at all. Why is this so? To begin with, the distance between a response utterance and its preceding stimulus is not usually very great. Out of 122 utterances in the H/L conversation, 18 were non-adjacent reactions – illustrated by this sequence, where U30 replies to U28:

28 L no news?
29 H then home by 1 for lunch
30 H not yet

Ten of the 18 non-adjacent reactions were separated by a single utterance in this way, and a further five by two utterances. Only three involved greater degrees of separation (one of which is illustrated above: U24 to U19), and there was no problem of miscomprehension.

An important factor is the sequencing of utterances. If N asks a question, N expects a reply, and is capable of waiting for that reply even though other utterances intervene. The intervening utterances typically do not cause ambiguity because they are grammatically and semantically unrelated. The relevant reply is signposted through the use of response grammar and by lexical items belonging to the semantic field of the question, as in this sequence:

150 N So will you be driving?
151 P I think Mike's going to be there.
152 P That'll make Jane smile.
153 P If the MOT's OK.

Participants even seem to cope with ambiguous anaphoric references and elliptical utterances, partly by remembering the linguistic context, but also by using their knowledge of the situation – something that is especially important in a situation where the participants know each other well. For example, U24 in the H/L dialogue could theoretically refer to U20, as it elides all reference to the activity; but both parties know that it could only refer to U19. Similarly, in U152 in the N/P dialogue, the *that* is theoretically ambiguous: it could refer to either the driving or to Mike. But as both participants know about the relationship between Mike and Jane, there is no problem.

If a participant feels that too much space has elapsed, several strategies are available to reaffirm semantic order, such as introducing the topic again. P, for example, could say:

P Driving? If the MOT's OK.

An example of this occurred in the H/L conversation, where after several utterances H returned to an earlier theme:

97 H re M – that's so exciting

This is especially likely to happen in forums, where several participants are involved and the time lag between messages is sometimes considerable. An observation submitted then has to have its target message identified, to avoid it being associated with the wrong utterance – for example, by inserting the name of the message-sender before a reply, as in 'Rob: I agree'. How many other such strategies are there? We need more studies of the techniques interactants use to maintain their sense of discourse organization in conversations involving multiple participants.

DIFFERENCES WITH WRITING

Hypertext links

The Internet is an association of computer networks with common standards which enable messages to be sent from any registered computer (or *host*) on one network to any host on any other. The mechanism which allows this to happen is the *hypertext link* – the colour-coded element on screen that users click on when they want to move from one part of the system to another. Hypertextuality is the most fundamental functional property of the Internet, without which the medium would not exist. It has parallels in some of the conventions of traditional written text – such as the footnote number, the cross-reference, and the bibliographical citation. These also motivate a reader to move from one place in a text to another. But they are optional features. It is perfectly possible to have a traditional text, such as a brochure, which has no footnotes or cross-references at all. It is not possible to have an Internet without hypertext links.

The hypertextuality in the current state of the Internet is of a very limited kind, dependent on the decisions made by individual site designers. In a fully hypertextual system, all documents would be completely and automatically interrelated. In the present system, links between sites are partial and often not reciprocated. Site X might link to site Y, but Y does not link to X. Nor does the existence of a link mean that it is achievable, as everyone knows who has encountered a 'page not found' error message. But technical issues aside, several linguistic questions arise. How should hypertext links be decided? It makes an interesting pedagogical exercise for a class to take a page of text and discuss, in an ideal hypertextual world, which elements would make the best links. A related exercise is to look at a real Internet page and evaluate whether links have been underused or overused. Just as we can over-footnote a traditional text, so we can over-link a web page. We need to ask how relevant or informative are the links on a page, and these are linguistic questions. Berners-Lee put it like this, when he wrote that the web 'is more a social creation than a technical one ... to help people work together'.[6] This seems to place the issue firmly within the remit of those parts of linguistics which deal with questions of discourse organization and audience – pragmatics, stylistics, and sociolinguistics.

Persistence

One of the most fundamental properties of traditional writing is its space-bound character – the fact that a piece of text is static and permanent on the page. If something is written down, repeated reference to it will be an encounter with an unchanged text. By contrast, a page on the web often varies: its factual content can change in front of our eyes, as when news headlines scroll across the screen or advertising pop-ups appear. This kind of dynamic or animated language is not restricted to the Internet – it has long been a feature of the neon signs in public advertising. What is different is the person-directed nature of the animation. We may even find a feature of our personal behaviour highlighted, as an ad colourfully informs us that we have won a huge sum of money.

Many web pages of course do have content which remains unchanged on repeated viewing – in a newspaper archive, for example, where the pages are an electronic replica of their printed original. But there are also many pages which have content that seems to be permanent, yet are found to have altered on subsequent viewing because they have been refreshed by the website-owner – as is routine with e-commerce pages, where the introduction of new models and prices provides the reader with content that is being continually updated. Outputs display different kinds of persistence. Comments to a website stay on a page for as long as the site exists, unless deleted for some reason by the website-owner. Messages are ephemeral on instant messaging unless a decision is made to log them. Emails stay until removed by the receiver (but may of course still be present on the host server). Archives of messages are routinely made in electronic mailing lists, blogs, and tweets.

User reactions to the content of a page also interfere with the traditional notion of the persistence of a written text. With several Internet categories, such as email, there are opportunities to 'interfere' with a message in ways that are not possible in traditional writing. A recipient may take a message and intercalate (or 'frame') responses to the various points that the sender made (see p. 73). The original sentences may be altered or deleted. In a chatroom or public forum, a third party might be involved, in the form of a moderator, whose role is to censor undesirable content. In all cases, the text can be modified with an ease and undetectability that is not possible when people try to alter a traditionally written text.

Multiple authorship

Intercalated and moderated texts illustrate a multi-authorship phenomenon which reaches its extreme in wiki-type pages, where readers may alter an existing text as their inclination takes them. The process raises important social and legal issues, but it also has several linguistic consequences.

First of all, it makes texts pragmatically heterogeneous, as the intentions behind the various contributions vary greatly. Wiki articles on sensitive topics (such as politics or religion) illustrate this most clearly, with judicious observations competing with contributions that range from mild through moderate to severe in the subjectivity of the writers' opinions. Texts are also stylistically heterogeneous. Sometimes there are huge differences, with standard and nonstandard language coexisting on the same page, often because some of the contributors are plainly communicating in a second language in which they are nonfluent. Traditional notions of stylistic coherence, with respect to level of formality, technicality, and individuality, no longer apply, though a certain amount of accommodation is apparent, with contributors sensing the properties of each other's style.

Cultural differences are especially important. People with different cultural backgrounds have different views on how formal a piece of writing on the Internet should be, or how focused or figurative it should be. One temperament requires that an author gets to the point quickly and stays focused on it; another requires a scene-setting preamble and allows diversions. One temperament is prone to vivid similes, metaphors, and personifications; another avoids them. In a setting such as Wikipedia, we find culture differences affecting the willingness of people to change a page – whether to add information, to clarify what is there, or to delete it. Some countries (such as Japan) seem to privilege editing; others (such as France) seem reluctant to interfere with the work of others.[7] The differences appear at a detailed level. We find pages which display a mix of contracted and uncontracted forms (e.g. *doesn't* vs *does not*), use conflicting conventions for writing dates, times, and addresses, or vary in their preferences over the use of colours. We need to know more about the diversity of expectations and behaviour among people from different cultures when they communicate on the Internet.

Multi-authorship also disturbs our sense of the physical identity of a text. How are we to define the boundaries of a text which is ongoing? People can now routinely add to a text posted online, either short-term, as in the immediate response to a news story, or medium- or long-term, as in comments posted to a blog, bulletin board, or other forum. Ferdinand de Saussure's classical distinction between synchronic and diachronic does not adapt well to the Internet, where everything is diachronic, time stampable to a micro-level. In classical linguistics, texts are typically viewed as synchronic entities, by which we mean we disregard the changes that were made during the process of composition and treat the finished product as if time did not exist. But with many Internet texts there is no finished product. I can today post a message to a forum discussion on page X created in 2004. From a linguistic point of view, we cannot say that we now have a new synchronic iteration of X, since the language has changed in the interim. I might comment that the discussion reads like something 'out of Facebook' – which is a comment that could be made only after 2005, when that network began.

The problem exists even when the person introducing the various changes is the same. The author of the original text may change it – altering a web page, or revising a blog posting. How are we to view the relationship between the various versions? The question is particularly relevant now that print-on-demand (POD) texts are becoming common. It is possible for me to publish a book very quickly and cheaply, printing only a handful of copies. Having produced my first print-run, I then decide to print another, but make a few changes to the file before I send it to the POD company. In theory (and probably increasingly common in practice), I can print just one copy, make some changes, then print another copy, make some more changes, and so on. The situation is beginning to resemble medieval scribal practice, where no two manuscripts were identical, or the typesetting variations between copies of Shakespeare's First Folio. The traditional terminology of 'first edition', 'second edition', 'first edition with corrections', ISBN numbering, and so on, is inadequate to account for the variability we now encounter; but it is unclear what to put in its place. The same problem is also present in archiving. The British Library, for example, launched a Web Archiving Consortium in 2008.[8] My website is included. But how is one to define the relationship between the various time-stamped iterations of this site, as they accumulate in the archive?

A NEW MEDIUM

The language of the Internet cannot be identified with either spoken language or written language, even though it shares some features with both. The electronic medium constrains and facilitates human strategies of communication in unprecedented ways. Among the constraints are limited message size, message lag, and lack of simultaneous feedback. Among the facilitations are hypertext links, emoticons, and the opportunities provided by multiple conversations and multiply authored texts. But this is only a partial account, which raises the general question: how many such design-features are there?

Susan Herring has approached this problem by adopting the notion of *facets* from the field of knowledge management.[9] Facets are parameters of contrast in relation to which outputs can be defined, and are similar in conception to the notion of design-features. Facets are grouped into two broad categories. *Technological facets* characterize the medium, determined by the associated computer hardware and software and by the character of the protocols governing the various outputs. *Social facets* characterize the number, relationship, and behaviour of those using the medium, the content and purpose of their communication, and the language they use.

Under the technological heading the following variables are recognized for online text (multimedia channels will need an extension of the approach):

- Synchronicity: whether the activity operates in real time (*synchronic*) or not (*asynchronic*)
- Granularity: the nature of the units transmitted by the system, whether messages, characters, or lines
- Persistence: the period of time that messages remain on the system after they are received
- Length: the number of characters that a system buffer allows in a single message
- Channels: the multimedia channels involved (animated graphics, video, audio)
- Identity: whether messages are anonymous or identified
- Audience: whether messages are publicly or privately accessible
- Adaptation: whether the system allows content to be filtered, quoted, or modified (cf. framing, p. 30)
- Format: the appearance of messages on screen, including such variables as the order in which they appear, their

location in relation to other messages, and whether other information is automatically appended

Under the heading of social facets, Herring identifies the following variables:

- Participation structure: the number of active or potential participants in an interaction, the amount they say, the speed at which they say it, whether they are interacting privately or public, and in real life or pseudo-life
- Participant characteristics: the usual range of factors identified by sociolinguists as relevant for language analysis, such as age, gender, education, cultural background, beliefs, and professional skills
- Purpose: the reason(s) for a message, whether sent by individuals or groups (e.g. playing a game, advertising a product, teaching a language)
- Activities: the means whereby the purpose is achieved (e.g. using text, sending photographs, adding sound, providing a forum)
- Topic: the kind of content felt to be relevant or appropriate to a message (cf. the common reference to a message being 'off-topic')
- Tone: the manner or spirit of an interaction (e.g. unemotional, jocular, aggressive, persuasive)
- Norms of organization: the way participants organize themselves (e.g. control content via a moderator, admit new members, distribute messages)
- Norms of social appropriateness: the behavioural standards accepted by the participants (e.g. netiquette guidelines, spam filters)
- Norms of language: the linguistic conventions recognized by participants (e.g. use of abbreviations, insider jokes, non-standard spellings)
- Code: the language(s) or language varieties used by the participants, whether spoken or written (i.e. including scripts and fonts)

Herring's list is an inventory, valuable as a tool for promoting the description and classification of Internet texts, within the various outputs. The next step is to collect corpora and carry out detailed descriptions, using parameters of this kind as guidelines. We can talk about the uniqueness of Internet language in general terms, but ultimately the only way to appreciate its character as a new medium is to carry out a linguistic investigation of a sample of data from an individual output. This invariably raises novel methodological issues, at the same time identifying features that are not encountered in analyses of 'traditional' speech and writing. A general account of the first Internet outputs – email, chat, virtual worlds, the web, instant messaging, blogging, and text-messaging – is already available in earlier works,[10] so for present purposes an apt illustration of the process can be found by taking a more recent development – an output whose linguistic origins lie in a combination of Internet and mobile phone.

See also 'Research directions and activities', pp. 151–3.

3

A MICROEXAMPLE: TWITTER

Twitter was the most rapidly growing Internet brand in 2010, with around 50 million tweets a day being posted during the first half of the year. Created in 2006, it is a microblogging platform that permits users to send and receive text-based posts (*tweets*) of up to 140 characters. Those who use the platform have no definitive group name, but *tweeters*, *twitterers*, *twits*, *tweople*, *twitizens*, *Twitter users*, and other forms are all found.

The figure of 140 arose because the aim was to allow users to read any tweet in its entirety, even if they were using a mobile phone, where messages are restricted to 160 (Roman alphabet) characters. (Twitter is sometimes described as 'the SMS of the Internet', as a consequence.) Twenty of the 160 characters were reserved for the user's name and associated symbols, leaving 140 visible characters to express message content. To help users work within this limit, the interface provides a counter showing how many characters have been used in a tweet. If a tweet exceeds the limit, it is automatically truncated, with the point of truncation shown by ellipsis dots (. . .).

Tweets are displayed on an author's profile page, are automatically delivered to those who have submitted an expression of interest in the author (*followers*), and can be read by anyone unless the author wishes to restrict delivery to a particular circle. A search of the Twitter database generates tweets displaying a two-part structure. The first element contains the author's identity and the message sent. The second part contains data about the tweet – its temporal source (related in real time to the moment of enquiry) and Internet origin – and response options. In its simplest form, a post on Twitter looks like this:

> stagewatch: just seen an excellent production of Macbeth at Shakespeare's Globe
> *4 days ago from web – Reply – View Tweet*

As Twitter evolved, it added several kinds of functionality. An @ symbol followed by a user name identifies the history of a semantic thread, signalling a reaction to a tweet on that user's page. So, if Fred wanted to respond to stagewatch, he might send this:

> Fred: @stagewatch I thought it was excellent too.

Retweeting is the process of forwarding a post from another user to all one's followers, usually using the abbreviation RT. The identity of the original author can be made explicit by prefixing RT to the username. This is how Fred would send the stagewatch message to his followers:

> Fred: RT @stagewatch just seen an excellent production of Macbeth at Shakespeare's Globe

These processes are iterative. A tweet can contain several RTs and @s, if the sender wants to give credit to all involved in originating the message. However, as the characters in user names all count towards the sender's 140 total, veteran tweeters recommend caution here. The more such references are included, the less room there is for fresh content.

The same problem arises if the sender appends a web source to the tweet. The URI (uniform resource indicator) of the theatre takes up 34 characters.

> Fred: RT @stagewatch just seen an excellent production of Macbeth at Shakespeare's Globe http://www.shakespeares-globe.org/

Some URIs are very much longer, so that tweets would soon exceed the 140 limit. To reduce this problem, automatic shortening techniques have been devised, such as the one currently used by Twitter from a US company, bit.ly. An address such as *http://www.exampleaddress.co.uk/suffix/anothersuffix.html* would be replaced by *http://bit.ly/xxxxxx*, where *xxxxxx* would be a unique sequence of letters and numerals. An option to expand the URI is available.

Other functional developments include the semantic grouping of posts by prefixing a term with a hash sign (#), the combination being known as a *hashtag*. *#language*, for example, would find all recent posts on the subject of language. Here is a real example (but with usernames changed), taken from a post which also contains three retweets:

> Tweeter1: RT @source1 RT @source2: RT @source3: Man invented language to satisfy his deep need to complain. ~ Lily Tomlin #quote #humor

A related semantic development was introduced in 2009 in the form of a sidebar which identifies frequency-based trends in the topics being tweeted. Also in 2009, a listing service was introduced, making it possible to organize followers into groups (such as the members of a family or colleagues in a company), thus enabling people to see a complete tweet stream from everyone in the list. In 2010, Google introduced a Twitter archiving service, and the Library of Congress announced plans to maintain a digital archive of all public tweets.

It is evident that the service is rapidly adapting to meet the needs and interests of users, so that linguistic generalizations are likely to date quickly.[1] But the core technological facets (as proposed by Herring, p. 33) can be summarized as follows:

- Synchronicity: asynchronic, but time-source is in real time (*4 days ago*)

- Granularity: message-based (*tweets*)
- Persistence: currently 3,200 tweets using Twitter, but with an archive of all tweets planned
- Length: 140 characters
- Channels: text, with an accompanying picture (author, logo, avatar)
- Identity: named, though often opaque (using nicknames, avatars)
- Audience: publicly accessible with optional restrictions
- Adaptation: forwarding (*retweets*), address shortening
- Format: new tweets at the top of the screen; messages embedded in a matrix of support information (see p. 42)

The sociolinguistic features are more difficult to identify, as the following microstudy will illustrate.

METHODOLOGICAL ISSUES

The language of any new Internet output takes time to settle down. Even with (relatively) long-established outputs, such as email, there continues to be considerable stylistic change (p. 11). With an output whose time-depth is less than four years (at the time of writing), we must expect to find a great deal of individual variation. However, the constraints of the technology will have motivated users to write in particular ways, so some tentative stylistic generalizations should be possible. Much will depend on the nature of the sample used for analysis, which in an initial enquiry need not be large but should represent many different users. It also makes sense to keep the sample as synchronic as possible, because contributions to a microblogging platform whose prompt is 'What's happening?' (p. 11) could be instantly affected by a fresh current of language change (such as a new catch-phrase). Stylistic features will also be more readily visible if the subject-matter is restricted. Twitter Search satisfies these criteria: by entering a single search term (*language*, in the present instance), I compiled a sample of 200 tweets within a 25-minute time frame, all from different authors.

Linguists investigating Internet outputs are continually having to address methodological issues. We could of course take a sample and describe every linguistic feature it contains – much as stylisticians have often done with extracts of everyday conversation or texts representing the language of science. But this would be to obscure one of the most important characteristics of Internet language: the distinction between the onscreen features that are automatically introduced by the software, over which the user has no control, and those features which are the result of linguistic choices made by the user. In the example above,

> stagewatch: just seen an excellent production of Macbeth at Shakespeare's Globe
> *4 days ago from web – Reply – View Tweet*

the first word and colon, and the final line, are elements introduced by the software. Only the sentence 'just . . . Globe' is from the user. And while both dimensions of usage need to be taken into account in the overall stylistic description of the output, the focus of linguistic interest has to be on the user's contributions, as it is only here that we will be able to address the kinds of variation recognized in a sociolinguistic checklist such as the one described by Herring.

With Twitter, methodological issues arise even within the user dimension. The phenomenon of retweeting introduces an element of repetitiveness in the data which is itself an important stylistic feature of Twitter, viewed as a language variety. Repetition is an unusual linguistic behaviour. It happens when adults talk to little babies, and it is an important language teaching strategy, but otherwise we do not repeat ourselves – or, if we do, it is considered a worrying sign (some types of language disorder, for example, are highly repetitive). So to find a variety where repetitive behaviour is a normal feature is noteworthy, and raises an interesting question. Should we include retweets in a description?

In my sample, 38 of the 200 posts (19 per cent) were retweets. Plainly, an account of some linguistic feature (e.g. the proportion of statements to questions) which included these repetitions would look very different from one which did not. The problem would be encountered in any output that privileges cutting and pasting, or copying and forwarding, such as email and networking forums, but Twitter is different. When I forward an email to you, it is usually accompanied by my own message explaining what I have done. In a forum, if I cut and paste an extract from an earlier post, it is to focus my ensuing comment. But with retweeting, the original post can be presented with nothing added. Some Twitter forums say that this is bad practice, and that retweets should always be accompanied by a comment from the sender, suggesting why the tweet was forwarded. If this were done, there would be a linguistic point in including the retweet, but in my sample this did not happen.[2] Fifteen of the retweets were slogans advocating a particular product, all of the form 'RT if you do X'. To include them would immediately produce an imbalance in the description (such as an unexpectedly high number of *if*-clauses). I therefore ignored all retweets with exact wording. However, this reduced the sample size by a fifth, to 162.

Further reductions in sample size had to be made. My aim was to draw conclusions about the linguistic character of Twitter using English as the medium of illustration. I had thought that the choice of a search term such as *language* would ensure that my sample would be safely monolingual. In fact three posts were written in other languages in which the English term happened to be used. They too had to be eliminated from the sample, which brought the total down to 159.

Twitter also presents us with the problem of what to do with incomplete utterances. It might be thought that tweeters would respect the 140-character convention, helped to do so by the counter which keeps a tally of the characters used as they compose a tweet. They do respect it, most of the time. Indeed, it is a point of pride with some tweeters to send a message that is exactly 140 characters in length (a *twoosh*, from the noise the system makes when such a post is achieved). But in 13 cases in my sample the tweet was truncated by the system, so that a sentence ends in mid-air, and the remainder of the message is lost. This is more likely to happen when a tweet is sent out automatically, as in the following example, where there has been no check on the length of the message (nor, it would seem, on formatting – the word spacing is reproduced exactly).

> JobsUK: #jobs #ruby Development Language expert: Salary/Rate: NegotiableLocation: CambridgeJob Title: Development Language . . . http://bit.ly/xxxxxx (expand)

Other cases include a post ending mid-verb phrase (*you should* . . .) or after an article (*the English language, a* . . .), making any further grammatical analysis impossible. All incomplete tweets were therefore eliminated from the sample, bringing the total down to 146. Incoherent or unwanted data is always a possibility when dealing with an electronic medium, but it is unusual to find as much as a quarter of a database (54 tweets out of my original 200) affected.

CONTENT ISSUES

As the earlier examples indicate, tweets are characterized by two kinds of material: a message element, which provides its primary linguistic content, and one or more optional identifiers (hashtags, @names, URIs) with a fixed internal structure. Only 40 of the 146 analysable tweets (27 per cent) consisted of a message element alone. The remainder incorporated between one and five identifiers, taking up between 5 and 44 per cent of the available character space (the 44 per cent case was the Tweeter1 example illustrated on p. 38). The average amount of space taken up by identifiers for all tweets in the sample was 20 per cent. Although identifiers are of less linguistic interest, they cannot be totally disregarded, because they may be incorporated into the grammar of the message, as these examples show:

> RT if your language is JONAS.

> Body language can influence an #interview.

> Just hearing of your influence on @HollywoodBan3U's unladylike use of language.

Tweeters do not make maximum use of the 140-character space, even when incorporating identifiers. (A similar trait can be seen in text-messaging, where it is unusual to find messages approaching the 160-character limit.) In my sample, there was just one example of a 140-character tweet, and the shortest example had only 29 characters. The average was 100.9 characters. It might be thought that character-count is linguistically irrelevant, but it can actually help to resolve an issue. The use of ellipsis dots to mark a truncation (p. 36) presents a possible ambiguity, as the same symbol is used with various other functions, such as indicating an omitted piece of text (as in a quotation), a hesitation, or an unfinished thought. Along with the dash, it is characteristic of informal writing, and tweets illustrate both – 15 tweets containing at least one dash, 25 containing at least one ellipsis, as in this example:

> Tweeter2: @ajmz language . . . somethign nontraditional . . . but dont know what yet . . . . just know i need the quote .

The number of dots and spaces is erratic, with some tweeters avoiding the use of a space on either side of the dots, and some reducing the number of dots to two, but in an example like this it is clear that the ellipses are linguistic in function, and nothing to do with truncation. It would also be clear in the following example, where the dots appear at the end:

> Tweeter3: I am not in a good mood, thanks to this poxy computer. . . . I will apologise now for language in the next tweet . . .

This has only 112 characters, so there is no question of truncation. The final dots have an unambiguously continuative function. However, the analysis becomes uncertain when the message approaches the length limit and the utterance appears to be grammatically complete, as in this 135-character example:

> Tweeter3: There's apparently lots of horrible grafitti and bad language getting scrawled all over the play area at Coquina . . . htt://bit.ly/xxxxxx

A decision has to be made whether to include such instances in the total of analysable sentences. (They *are* included in the further comments below.)

The pressure to convey information within the length constraint results in users adopting a variety of shortening techniques. Writers on Twitter forums recommend several strategies, such as the use of contractions, logograms (e.g. *&* for *and*), abbreviations, the use of single (not double) spaces at sentence ends, elliptical sentences (e.g. omitting *I* as a subject), and a range of relevant but vague avoidance principles, such as 'leave out unnecessary words' or 'omit unnecessary punctuation marks'.[3] These strategies could all be seen in my sample, though few were frequent. Where the choice between a contracted and a noncontracted form was possible, contractions were the definite usage of choice (59 out of 79 instances, 75 per cent). Logograms were not common, however, with just six instances being used by three tweeters. Emoticons were a little more frequent, but the frequency was of the same order as has been noted in some other Internet outputs (15 instances, 10 per cent). The same point applied to abbreviations, which occurred in only 25 tweets (17 per cent) – and over half of these (13) were *lol*. Thirty-one tweeters (21 per cent) went in for logograms (&, +, 1, 2, 3) or shorter nonstandard respellings – *n* [and], *u/ur* [you(r)], *dat* [that], *das* [that is], *ppl* [people], *favs* [favourites], *wen* [when], *wat* [what], *ova* [over], *dnt* [don't], *knw* [know], *thx* [thanks], *tho*[ugh], *gf* [girlfriend], *diff*[erence], and three instances of a dropped final *-g*, as in *doin*. Although none of these strategies is individually frequent, their cumulative effect is to make the tone of this variety predominantly informal (an exception is the block language of announcements, illustrated on p. 49).

We might expect punctuation to be the area where it is easiest to save some characters. There is no linguistic need to end a tweeted statement with a period, for example, as the fact that the message is finished is obvious from the way it is graphically presented. The primary purpose of a sentence-final period is to separate sentences in the sort of continuous text that Twitter is not designed to display. What is surprising, therefore, is to see traditional punctuation conventions generally respected. Excluding the cases ending with ellipsis dots, 108 tweets in my sample (74 per cent) had final punctuation. In 41 cases (28 per cent) a statement ended with a period. In 32 cases the utterance concluded with an exclamation mark (21 occurrences, with the mark sometimes repeated – in one case, as many as five times) or question mark (11 occurrences, with the mark also sometimes repeated). In 4 cases the utterance ended with a colon, whose function was to introduce the final URI. There were also occasional unusual combinations of marks, such as --*!* and *?* ... Of the 51 cases (35 per cent) where tweets lacked conventional marks, 8 concluded with *lol* or an emoticon, and 12 with a URI. If we interpret these as having some sort of sentence-marking function, we are left with only 31 cases (21 per cent) where a tweet ended with no punctuation at all.

GRAMMATICAL ISSUES

When we examine the internal grammatical structure of tweets, we encounter a problem. The combination of shortening techniques plus the use of nonstandard punctuation makes it difficult at times to assign a definite syntactic analysis to the utterance. We often encounter a series of sentential fragments, as in the following examples:

> you can but you won't get a job – instead talk about work/life balance – same issue business bullshit language:

> Language packs for Windows XP Service Pack 3 – Full: Windows Software

There were 36 cases of this kind in my sample (25 per cent), containing between one and four fragments. They were especially noticeable in advertisements and announcements. While several of these fragments display coherent structure at phrase or clause level, words are sometimes juxtaposed in a way which makes an immediate interpretation impossible (*same issue business bullshit language*). It is likely, of course, that such strings would become clear when they are seen in context within the writers' tweet stream; but for samples of the present kind, they remain resistant to analysis.

A decision also has to be made about how to handle minor sentences (*yeah, wow, hey, haha*, etc.), which are a noticeable feature of Twitter data.[4] Presumably elements such as *lol, omg, btw, smh*, and emoticons should be classed as minor sentences, even though some etymologically represent something more complex (*laughing out loud, scratching my head*). These appear in 25 tweets (17 per cent) and are a major feature of the style of some tweeters, who can introduce three or four in a single message:

> ha ha yea thats the best language to speak lol

In all, 36 tweets (25 per cent) incorporate minor sentences of one kind or another.

At the same time, there are tweets where the sentences would be classed as major and 'complete' in any description:

> i cant help but be amazed how my classmate can communicate with sign language. its truly remarkable

This is an example where there are two sentences – a common tweet pattern. Of 118 tweets where sentences were easily analysable in this way, 50 consisted of a single sentence, 49 of two, 15 of three, and 4 of four. Ellipsis of the subject (and auxiliary verb) was common in sentences following the opening one, but even the first sentence can be elided, reflecting the generally informal tone of the output:

> Did really well on my Spanish presentation. hoping that it will help me get out of taking language again. Just need to do well on the final?

Average sentence length was 7.1 words. (The average number of words per tweet was 14.7, with a very wide range, from 2 – a brief announcement – to 28.) This is actually quite high – higher than we find in instant messaging, for example[5] – and reflects the fact that some tweets display sentences of considerable complexity. Examples such as the following illustrate the point, and refute the claim made by critics of this output that Twitter forces a simple syntax on its users:

> Sign language, like English, evolves as people create new signs when no sign exists, or when new technology or cultural events develop.

> That ridiculous language wouldn't be necessary if AZ would've been allowed to do something about people being there illegally

> I had 2tell some kids 2day wen they get older&go job interviews they cant speak yoyoyo bitch & dog language wen they greet their interviewer

Other signs of grammatical complexity exist, in the form of pointers to higher levels of discourse organization. The original Twitter prompt, 'What are you doing?', would have elicited a high proportion of utterances that were grammatically and semantically self-contained. A small sample I made of tweets when they first appeared showed a preponderance of self-contained utterances, initiating a topic:

> Missed the bus and got to work late. Grr!

> Beautiful day here in London.

> Am stuck in a lift.

Occasionally there would be some self-reference:

> Missed the bus again. Must get up earlier.

But there was no real sense of dialogue between tweeters, and only hints of emerging semantic threads. My 2010 sample is different, as these examples suggest:

> So it's not just the English language that's suffering bastardization . . .

> That probably means something in another language

> lol yeah I wasn't thinking fast enough!

> I agree!!!! hahaha

Here we get a clear sense of an ongoing monologue or dialogue. In 55 cases (38 per cent) the tweets contain some marker of grammatical cohesion – in many instances, more than one:

- conjunctions: *and*, *but*, *cos*
- connecting adverbs: *so*, *well*, *as well*, *also*
- response utterances: *lol*, *yeah*, *ok*, *thx*, *I agree*, *hahaha*, *:)*
- clarificatory utterances: *I meant . . ., really?*
- anaphoric forms: *that is a shame*, *it's one of my favs*
- direct address forms: *hey girl*, *you/u*, *your*
- commands: *cheer up*, *mind your language*
- direct questions: *is that some kinda different language?*

This may partly be a direct consequence of the change of prompt from 'What are you doing?' to 'What's happening?' in November 2009 (p. 11). It is not possible at present to examine earlier tweets to see the extent to which markers of cohesion were already appearing before the change. This could be an interesting diachronic study, once the data becomes available.

PRAGMATIC ISSUES

It is evident, from this last set of examples, that a linguistic analysis of Twitter cannot restrict itself to matters of formal sentence description: a pragmatic perspective is essential. Pragmatics, within linguistics, always tries to provide explanations for uses of language: what factors govern a person's choice of utterance? what are the effects of that choice on an addressee? In Herring's list of social facets (p. 35) we are dealing chiefly with purpose and tone.

It might be thought that a pragmatic classification of tweets would be straightforward, given that there is a prompt motivating user response. In fact, neither of the recognized prompts elicited many associated responses. There were only 21 cases in my database (14 per cent) where the tweet was clearly a response to 'What are you doing?' (and these included utterances which stretch the 'present time' implication somewhat, to allow for events that are of current relevance):

in language arts watching a movie . . . haha

Trying out my language skills by doing a sudoku in a Swedish paper

just finished my Greek lesson.

I am delivering my thesis presentation tomorrow . . .

A similar number were analysed as answering the question 'What's happening?', the responses including factual statements of a general kind alongside news reporting and announcements:

Italian Word of the Day: Tempo

Ancient language discovered at Teotihuacan in Mexico

Coma Victim's Language Ability Explained: Discovery News

As always with pragmatic classifications, there are many cases that are marginal or uncertain. Depending on our view about current relevance, some 'What doing?' utterances might be classified as 'What's happening?' And the latter category is not entirely clear cut. 'What's happening?' is a request to provide information. Should we then include under this heading tweets which themselves ask for information or help, or provide responses to such requests?

We are looking for Norwegian language translators.

spell check options then language settings and click the 'spell check' box

However, if these *are* included, and we combine 'What doing?' and 'What happening?' tallies, we still only get a total of 28 per cent. Other factors seem to be more important in explaining the communicative function of tweets.

The largest category in my database (61 cases, 39 per cent) consisted of observations or opinions, including the opinions of others as represented through aphorisms and quotations:

> Election language is making less & less sense to me.
>
> How can a nation be UNITED when all of its citizens can't even speak the same language?
>
> A way of life dies with the death of a language
>
> colloquialism is wat keeps a language alive

The next most frequent category (27 cases, 17 per cent) was advertising, in the broadest sense to include products, services, and want ads.

> Free Sci-fi ebook: The Graveyard of Space: Author: Stephen Marlowe Language: English
>
> Free webinar! [*followed by a long URI*]
>
> Speech Language Pathologist – Per Diem – Home Health Job

If retweets were included in an analysis, this figure would increase significantly.

That leaves a group of tweets whose function seems to be the building or breaking of rapport, or the creating or maintaining of a social atmosphere. They are sometimes dismissed by commentators as 'pointless babble', as in a 2009 survey carried out by Pear Analytics,[6] but that displays a misunderstanding of the nature of conversation, and especially of those aspects of communication which have been variously referred to as 'gossip', 'phatic communion', or 'social cement'.

> hahahaha . . . ur using weird language!!
>
> I know girl . . . smh good thing I know Sign Language!!
>
> I'm sorry if I just offended you in a different language
>
> ??i dont get ur language

In the Pear survey, some 40 per cent of the sample was assigned to this category. In mine the figure was only 16 per cent, but this will probably have been due to my sampling criterion: a search using the term *language* is likely to come up with a higher proportion of non-gossipy utterances.

A fault with many popular surveys is that they fail to take into account unclear cases and the multiple functions that a tweet can express. The Pear survey, for example, classified tweets into news, spam, self-promotion, pointless babble, conversational, and pass-along value. Several arbitrary decisions must have been made in the process, in view of tweets from my sample such as the following:

> I am in language arts so boring:/ [a combination of What doing? + Opinion]

> Enjoy! Love the sumptuous language of R&J. I'll be in Stratford in May to see Antony and Cleopatra. [a combination of Rapport + Opinion + What happening?]

The recommendation (p. 41) that additional content should be added to retweets also indicates the importance of multiple functions. And the pragmatic force of such forms as *lol* and emoticons especially needs to be taken into account. There is a world of difference between an advertising tweet which simply says 'buy this product' and a retweet which says 'buy this product lol' or 'buy this product :D'. However we interpret the final element, whether positively or negatively, it is plain that an attitude is being expressed that is not part of the original advertisement, and this should be reflected in any pragmatic analysis.

Similarly, we have to recognize that any classification of communicative functions is bound to raise problems of analysis because not everyone understands functional labels in the same way. It is a classical criticism of speech act categories that even apparently simple labels such as 'request' and 'persuade' can be given widely different applications in a sample of utterances. Any analysis has to allow a category of 'unclear', to handle those cases where there is insufficient context to make a definite assignment.

A VARIETY IN EVOLUTION

The aim of a variety analysis in sociolinguistics or stylistics is to determine the extent to which a particular use of language displays features that uniquely identify it as belonging to a particular social situation, and differentiate it from the kind of language used in other situations. The features introduced by Twitter technology readily characterize this output as a variety: no other use of language combines identity and message in the way that tweets do, or displays messages with the kind of internal structure illustrated above. But a full description of the stylistic features of Twitter remains a goal of future research, because much larger samples of data will be needed to establish the trends that are currently obscured by individual variation and the output's ongoing evolution. It is not really possible yet to say much about norms of language and social appropriateness, for example (cf. Herring's list of social facets, p. 35), and information about participant background will require a fuller analysis of user profiles than is currently available; but certain trends have been indicated by academic and industry surveys.[7]

Several reports consistently indicate a female majority in Twitter users. One survey, by Nielsen Mobile (April 2009), found 57 per cent female use; another (November 2009) found 59 per cent female use; and a Business Insider report (April 2010) found 53 per cent.[8] Some commentators on these reports saw this result as unsurprising, saying that it simply reflects the greater tendency for women to engage in social chat. However, without a correlation of gender with the functional distinctions described above (where, for example, social chat accounted for only 16 per cent of the tweets in my sample), it is not safe to draw such a conclusion. In any case, gender identification is not a straightforward matter, as tweeters do not give this information in their profiles, and the avatars they choose are often unrevealing. One study deduced gender by a comparison with name lists where the gender was known, but we cannot take Twitter names at face value. Fake profiles are an unknown (but probably significant) element.

Industry surveys have also begun to provide data on the age demographic, with results that have surprised commentators, who were expecting it to reflect the young person profile found in the early days of text-messaging and still seen in some social networking sites. In fact, young people (under-18s) are a small minority on Twitter, constituting just 11 per cent of users in an August 2009 survey. The majority of users are above age 35: 49 per cent in that survey, and 64 per cent in another survey in February 2010.[9] If this bias is maintained, it suggests that young people are less concerned with the news and information functions which are Twitter's primary motivation, and more concerned with the establishment and maintenance of identity, which is chiefly associated with such social networking agencies as Facebook through the opportunity to join interest groups, state personal interests, give contact information, and so on.

Data on usage patterns are also of linguistic interest, as they bear directly on the general communicative character of the output. Twitter does not seem to be a type of social network in which conversational dialogue and group cohesion predominate. According to a *Harvard Business Review* study (May 2009), the typical Twitter user contributes to the network infrequently, the median number of lifetime tweets per user being 1. A large percentage of Twitter accounts are inactive. This impression is reinforced in a later survey (January 2010) which reported that around 25 per cent of accounts had no followers, and about 40 per cent had never sent a single tweet.[10] About 80 per cent of users tweeted fewer than 10 times. Over 50 per cent of users tweeted less than once every 74 days. These usage patterns are very different from other online social networks.

On the other hand, a small group of users are extremely active. The Harvard study found that the top 10 per cent of tweeters accounted for over 90 per cent of all tweets, contrasting with other social networks, where the top 10 per cent accounted for 30 per cent of all production. The pattern far more resembles what has been found for Wikipedia, where 15 per cent of the most prolific editors account for 90 per cent of the edits. Wikipedia is plainly not a conversational medium, which suggests that Twitter's primary function is more a publishing service or a medium of self-expression, in which one user informs many people, rather than a dialogue among peers. In my sample, over

80 per cent of the tweets were reports, opinions, and advertisements, which locates the output at some remove from outputs whose primary function is social networking.

In 2007, Twitter was being used by some half a million people. By mid-2008 this had risen to 2 million; by mid-2009 to 14 million; by the end of 2009 to 75 million; and by April 2010 to over 100 million. Given such a remarkable rate of development over such a short time frame, it is likely that generalizations about usage will change, as has been found in relation to other outputs (p. 11). Conclusions about its social character remain tentative, therefore. Already there is considerable debate about Twitter content. On the negative side, commentators have criticized message banality and self-indulgence, spam levels, and inappropriate messages (such as tweeting about a job application or at a funeral). On the positive side, there has been praise for the way the output provides real-time updates about breaking news (such as about an impending hurricane) and offers an additional level of commentary about public events, as the following anecdote illustrates.

After giving a lecture at a media conference in Florida in 2009, I was shown my 'Twitter score' by the organizer – the number of people in my audience who had tweeted while I was lecturing (using a hashtag that had been set up specially for the occasion). The tweets were various: some were quotes of what I had said; some offered opinions about what I said. A few actually discussed what I had said, when members of the audience reacted to each other's tweets. Already, people who were not at the conference (but who were aware that it was taking place) were reading the tweets; and soon after the conference, the tweets were attracting a wide readership. This is a new phenomenon. Instead of writing notes about an event for our own private purposes, we can now send these directly to the Internet. People who do not have the opportunity to ask questions or express their opinions about an event can do so, succinctly. And I suspect it is only a matter of time before Twitter feeds are routinely incorporated into a podium, so that speakers can follow (if they wish) reactions while they are coming in. The possibilities are intriguing. Will live theatre audiences tweet? Might actors on stage ever be tempted to follow the tweets being written by those in front of whom they are currently performing? And, if they did, what would the effect be?

A question which looms large in the popular mind, whenever a new Internet output is encountered, is whether the output is causing changes in our communicative behaviour. Already claims are being made that the 140-character limit of Twitter is changing our ways of thinking – or perhaps, more precisely, reinforcing a change in attention span that is already taking place as a result of texting, instant messaging, and surfing. Nicholas Carr put it like this:[11]

> Over the past few years I've had an uncomfortable sense that someone, or something, has been tinkering with my brain, remapping the neural circuitry, reprogramming the memory. My mind isn't going – so far as I can tell – but it's changing. I'm not thinking the way I used to think. I can feel it most strongly when I'm reading. Immersing myself in a book or a lengthy article used to be easy. My mind would get caught up in the narrative or the turns of the argument, and I'd spend hours strolling through long stretches of prose. That's rarely the case anymore. Now my concentration often starts to drift after two or three pages. I get fidgety, lose the thread, begin looking for something else to do. I feel as if I'm always dragging my wayward brain back to the text. The deep reading that used to come naturally has become a struggle. . . . I'm not the only one. When I mention my troubles with reading to friends and acquaintances – literary types, most of them – many say they're having similar experiences. The more they use the Web, the more they have to fight to stay focused on long pieces of writing.

The claims are controversial. Exploring the basis of this feeling, and providing much-needed evidence, is undoubtedly going to be a major focus of future psycholinguistic research.

People have also wondered whether the Internet is having an impact on the character of individual languages. The question of language change is never far away, when the Internet is being discussed. Have languages developed novel linguistic features or lost traditional ones, as a result of Internet activity? All new technologies – writing, printing, telephony, radio, television, etc. – cause language change, and motivate reactions which range from celebration to antagonism. One of the most important roles of Internet linguistics is to establish exactly what these changes are. In particular, are they as widespread as many people think?

See also 'Research directions and activities', p. 153.

4

LANGUAGE CHANGE

How much linguistic change has taken place since the arrival of the Internet? The phenomenon is so recent – few people would be able to acknowledge its presence in their lives before the mid-1990s – that we might expect very little to have happened. Changes in language typically take decades, or even lifetimes, before they are established. But history is no guide, when it comes to electronic technology. In olden times (i.e. before the Internet), it would take several years before a new word would achieve a sufficiently high community profile to appear in print, be picked up by lexicographers, and come to be recorded in dictionaries. Today, a new word can achieve a global profile within hours. It seems likely that the Internet will speed up the process of language change.

But so far the effect of the Internet on the character of individual languages has been very limited. If we take a cursory look at an instance of Internet language, such as an email, a web page, a blog, or a tweet, the initial impression is that little has changed. We will notice the occasional novel usage, but on the whole the individual words, grammatical constructions, and orthographic patterns seem to be little different from what we observe in language used outside the electronic medium. However, 'little difference' is not the same as 'no difference'. An important initial task of Internet linguistics is therefore to provide a description of the way vocabulary, grammar, graphology, and pragmatics are being used in novel ways within the various outputs. A future task will be to do the same thing for phonology.

VOCABULARY

Because of its role as a primary index of culture, vocabulary is always the area of language that most readily manifests change. And of all the domains of culture represented within a lexicon, science and technology play a particularly important role, making up (according to some estimates) over 70 per cent of the words in an unabridged dictionary.[1] So we might expect that, with such a hugely innovative technology as the Internet, we will find a significant number of new words.

The focus has to be on words that have arisen directly as a result of the Internet, and which are encountered when someone is involved in any of its outputs. Terms such as *computer*, *software*, *monitor*, *cable*, *byte*, *crash*, and *freeze* need to be excluded, as they are not specifically Internet terms, having an independent and prior use in electronics and computer science. By contrast, terms such as *blog*, *blogging*, and *blogger* are clear candidates, referring as they do to situations, activities, and people that only exist because of the Internet. Each Internet output has its own terminology, encountered first in the presentation of its functionality on screen, and later in the linguistic innovations introduced by its users, such as slang and playful adaptation. In the absence of large corpora of Internet vocabulary, it is currently impossible to say how frequently a neologism is used, other than through the linguistically untrustworthy approximations provided by search engine counts (untrustworthy, because they fail to tag search words for word-class, discount redundancy arising out of page duplication, or distinguish pages belonging to different time frames). In addition, many neologisms are nonce-usages, invented by users as a whim, and achieving no presence on the Internet beyond the individual's own website. An unknown number will have become obsolete. But the examination of individual neologisms can nonetheless provide revealing hints about the evolution of the Internet lexicon.

The emergence of a new area of Internet activity always generates a great deal of enthusiastic neologizing, and this takes a while to settle down. In 2010, around 600 neologisms were listed in Twittonary, one of the online dictionaries collecting terms that have been invented in connection with Twitter. That is quite a total, for a period of less than five years. However, when we examine them closely, we find that the vast majority are the result of people exploiting the wordplay possibilities of the name, especially those suggested by the unusual (in English) phonetic properties of the initial consonant cluster [tw-]. Two-thirds of the entries are plays on that cluster, usually by replacing an initial consonant (*twictionary*, *tweologism*, *tweckling*) or [tr-] (*twendy*, *twaffic*), or by adding an extra initial cluster (*twidentity theft*, *twaddiction*, *twissues*). Blends are also very common (*twittersphere*, *twitterhea*, *twitterati*, *twitterholic*, *celebritweet*). Most of these are likely to have a short linguistic life. Just a few will be long-term additions to the language – or, at least, for as long as Twitter exists. Which words live or die, and which factors promote their life or death, must be important questions for historical lexicology.

Diachronic investigations of the structure of an output's semantic field can benefit from being comparative. We can, for example, compare Twitter terminology with that belonging to an output that has been around for much longer – blogging. In the early 2000s, this too generated a great deal of wordplay, but online dictionaries today contain only a fraction of the neologisms that were being circulated then. What is interesting is to see the same linguistic processes in operation. We find the same sort of substitution of clusters (*blargon* 'blog jargon') and syllables (*blogathy* 'blog apathy') and a similar range of blends (*blogosphere*, *blogorrhea*, *blogerati*, *blogoholic*, *celebriblog*). The unique phonetic properties of the core term are again exploited: internal rhyme is seen in *bloggerel*, *lexiblography*, and *blogstipation* (the sad state of affairs when a blogger can't think of anything to say). Rather more technical are such blends as *blogroll* and *blogware*, *photoblog* and *moblog* ('posts sent by mobile phone'), or *blawg* ('law blog') and *vlog* ('video blog'), and such compounds as *blog client* and *blog archive*. It is terms of this latter kind which seem to have achieved a long-term place in the language – though again, this will be the case for only as long as the technology exists. Important too are well-established words which have been given a new sense in the context of blogging, such as *gadget*, *post*, *preview*, *archive*, and *template*.

Looking at Internet vocabulary as a whole, we immediately see terms associated with the software functionality which enables people to use the medium. They often appear on screen in the form of labels used to designate screen areas and operations, and to specify user options and commands. We find old words with new applications, such as *edit*, *help*, *format*, *tools*, *font*, *menu*, *preferences*, *options*, *palette*, *bookmark*, and *zoom*, as well as new collocations such as *track changes*, *data merge*, *print preview*, *undo typing*, and the different kinds of *error message* (such as *404 file not found*). Some forms have been especially productive, such as *cyber-*, *hyper-*, *e-*, *web-*, *-bot*, and *-ware*. Abbreviations, always a characteristic of technology, are a very frequent feature, as seen in hundreds of acronyms such as *URL* ('uniform resource locator'), *FAQ* ('frequently asked question'), and *WWW* ('World Wide Web'), as well as in the suffixes that form the top level of the domain name system, such as *doc*, *com*, *org*, *co*, *uk*, *us* (USA), and *de* (Germany).[2]

Plainly the Internet is lexically highly active and rapidly changing. Yet, if we were to count all the items that have come into a language as a result of Internet activity, we would be talking about only a few thousand – and many of these, as suggested above, are playful nonce-formations. When we compare this with the terminology found in botany or chemistry – subjects which use tens of thousands of technical terms – we have to conclude that the Internet is as yet playing a relatively minor role in the character of a language's lexicon. In the case of English, where the lexicon runs to well over a million items, an extra few thousand new items from the domain of the Internet is hardly of great significance. Certainly there are no lexical grounds for saying, as media pundits sometimes do, that Internet vocabulary has been a radical source of language change. All that has happened is that languages have acquired an additional lexical dimension, as they always do when their speakers gain a new domain of knowledge.

We come to the same conclusion when we look for cases where Internet terminology has had an influence on everyday speech and writing. There are indeed a number of words which have developed alternative senses of a nontechnical kind when used figuratively in conversation. Examples include *download* as a noun in the sense of 'full report' (*Give me a download of what's going on*), *offline* as an adjective in the sense of 'unavailable' (*The flu's going to keep him offline for a few days*), and *hack* as a verb in the sense of 'solve' (*I've hacked it – the fuse has blown*). But in a 2004 glossary I was able to find only about 70 such extensions,[3] and, while a few others have made their appearance since then, the overall total remains low. The same point applies to Internet abbreviations: only a tiny number are heard outside of the domain of electronic communication – *LOL* ('laughing out loud') being the most widespread English example, heard both as an acronym [el o: el] and as a word [lol]. Playful linguistic encodings, such as those deriving from the use of the same sequence of keystrokes in predictive texting (saying *book* instead of *cool*) or the substitution of ASCII characters for roman letters (as in *l33t* 'leet'), tend to be restricted to individual Internet groups, only occasionally providing expressions that are taken up by the wider community. All these developments form an interesting area of study within Internet lexicology, but one which so far is quite limited in scope.

ORTHOGRAPHY

When people look for novel linguistic features on the Internet, it is usually the orthography which first catches their attention. At one extreme they see an enhanced system – web pages using a range of fonts and formats, a variety of colours, and elements of animation. At the other extreme they see a reduced system – messages which omit punctuation, avoid capital letters, and have little or no typographical contrastivity. It is the reduced system which has attracted most attention, because some people see the use of nonstandard forms as a symptom of decline in educational and linguistic standards, and are vociferous in their condemnation. But a focus on extremes tells only part of the story of Internet graphology, and one of the tasks of Internet linguistics is to describe the range of orthographic forms that are used in the various outputs, and to establish the factors that give rise to them.

The situation turns out to be quite complex. What factors might promote the use of nonstandard spelling, capitalization, or punctuation? It could be any of several reasons. The writers might be ignorant of the standard usage. They might know it, but not be bothered to use it. They might be bothered, but don't have keyboard skills up to the task of typing it correctly. They might think they've typed it correctly, when actually they haven't, and failed to read their message through before sending it. They might make a conscious decision not to bother with the standard form, because they feel it is unimportant. They might, consciously or unconsciously, use the nonstandard form in order to accommodate to the usage of their peers. They might deliberately use it to create a special effect. Or some combination of these factors might apply. In all cases, age, gender, educational background, linguistic taste, and personality influence the outcome. Trends are apparent. Older people – but not all – tend to be linguistically more conservative than younger. Women – but not all – tend to use more punctuation marks than men.[4] We need many more sociolinguistically informed studies.

The counting of individual forms is in any case only part of the research task. Much more important are the functions (semantic and pragmatic) that these forms express. An illustration is the observation that women use more exclamation marks than men, as has been noted in relation to various outputs. Because of the widely recognized function of the exclamation mark as a sign of increased emotional intensity, it would be easy to draw the conclusion that female messages are more emotive than male. But when a functional analysis is made of exclamation marks, such a conclusion is demonstrably naive. One such study distinguished a wide range of exclamatory functions, as observed in discussion groups, such as the following:[5]

- An action, or call to action, by the individual posting the message, e.g. *Read eBooks!*
- An implied or direct apology, e.g. *My apologies!*
- A challenge or dare, e.g. *Prove it!*
- An expression of agreement or support, e.g. *You're right!*
- A statement of fact, e.g. *It turned my hair grey!*
- A self-disclosure, e.g. *My hair is getting grey!*
- An opinion, e.g. *I like Blackboard!*
- A friendly greeting or closure, e.g. *Hi!*, *Good luck!*
- An expression of annoyance, rudeness, or hostility, e.g. *I told you – no!*, *You jerk!*
- An attempt to avoid tension, e.g. *Calm down!*
- A sarcastic remark, e.g. *Big deal!*
- An expression of thanks, e.g. *Thanks for that!*

The study confirmed the previously reported bias, with 73 per cent of all exclamations being made by females. But only 19 (9.5 per cent) of the exclamations expressed excitability. Far more were used for other functions, such as markers of friendly interaction (32 per cent), including thanking, or to emphasize a statement of fact (29.5 per cent). The author concludes that exclamation marks are more an indication of supportiveness rather than emotionality.

The situation is no less complex at a descriptive level. It is an oversimplification to say that people who use a reduced orthographic system in one message will always do so in others – or even that they will always do so within the same message. Much depends on the content. If the writer is making a statement, there may well be no period at the end; but if it is a question or an exclamation, there will usually be the appropriate mark. Indeed, with emotional content, the number of marks can increase rather than decrease, as this instant messaging exchange illustrates:

A   hope you can make the party
B   yes i can
A   fantastic!!!!

Apparent inconsistency in the use of punctuation can also reflect an awareness of difficulty, as this example suggests:

> we're on the train
> i'll ask him

This is from a writer who also used these forms:

> he isnt coming
> why cant he

Why does the writer insert an inverted comma in *we're* and *i'll*? Perhaps because he senses that the apostrophe makes the sentences easier to read. Compare the effect without the apostrophe:

> were on the train
> ill ask him

These sentences are not ambiguous: the context makes it clear what is meant. But it takes a moment longer for us to process them, as the homographs *were* and *ill* momentarily lead us – as some linguists put it – up the wrong garden path.

Capitalization is another area where there is a great deal of variation. Most of the Internet is not case sensitive, so there is a strong tendency to use lower-case everywhere, avoiding the extra awkwardness (for most amateur typists) involved in choosing the upper-case option on a keyboard. The lower-case default mentality means that any use of capitalization is a strongly marked form of communication. Messages entirely in capitals are considered to be 'shouting', and netiquette guides strongly recommend they should be avoided. But do people respect these guidelines? And if they do, what alternative graphological conventions do they use to express the semantic function of capitals, such as for emphasis? Asterisks, spacing, and boldface are all available:

> I was REALLY excited
> I was *really* excited
> I was r e a l l y excited
> I was **really** excited

But it is unclear how widely these variants are used, or whether people make subtle systematic distinctions between them.

A distinctive feature of Internet graphology is the way capitals are used within words – a phenomenon variously called *bicapitalization (BiCaps)*, *intercaps*, *incaps*, or *midcaps*. It is quite a common practice in proper names, as in *AltaVista*, *EarthLink*, *CompuServe*, *QuarkXPress*, and *aRMadillo Online*, but rarely seen elsewhere. Another innovation is the use of symbols borrowed from programming languages, such as an initial exclamation mark to express negation (*!interesting = not interesting*). Sometimes a specialized symbol achieves a popular presence, as with the use of hash (#) to identify semantic threads in Twitter (p. 38); but usually such symbols are seen only in exchanges among people with a technical background. They are not a major factor in language change.

We might expect to see rather more change taking place in the spelling system, especially in languages that display a considerable number of variants or irregular forms. In the case of English, the variants (*judgment* vs *judgement*, *color* vs *colour*, *encyclopedia* vs *encyclopaedia*, *flowerpot* vs *flower-pot* vs *flower pot*, etc.) have several origins, such as different preferences in British and American English or different choices made by printers and publishers. A considerable proportion of English vocabulary is affected: one estimate found that over 5 per cent of the words in a college-sized dictionary offered alternative forms.[6] Which variants do people choose? The choices they make are partly conditioned by their educational background, but are also influenced by what they see used around them. Young people today see more written language on the Internet than anywhere else. It is inevitable, therefore, that spelling trends observed on the Internet will sooner or later shape people's intuitions about what is permissible, and feed back into the writing system as a whole.

Search-engine counts are useful in investigating spelling because they are a reasonably accurate guide to exposure. It does not matter whether *jail* is being used as a noun or a verb, appears on duplicate pages, or is found in pages spanning several years. The point is simply: which of the alternatives (*jail* or *gaol*) are people more exposed to when they explore the Internet? The answer for this choice, and for several others, is shown in Table 4.1, using 2010 Google totals rounded to the nearest million. The totals do not distinguish cases where different spellings are associated with different meanings (*computer programs* exist alongside *television programmes* in British English), but they are nonetheless suggestive. The hypothesis would be that Variant 2 items with small frequencies towards the top of Table 4.1 are more likely to become obsolete than items further down.

Similarly, we can investigate growth in nonstandard spellings. All the items in column 3 of Table 4.2 are errors in standard English, but they display great variations in frequency on the Internet. Several of the nonstandard forms have been proposed by supporters of spelling reform, as a means of simplifying the system. Up until now, with the exception of Noah Webster's revision of spelling for American English, reform proposals have come to nothing. It may well be that Internet users, voting (as it were) with their fingers, will introduce simplifications of the kind the reform movement has long desired, such as the dropping of silent letters. If so, then the hypothesis would be that an everyday word such as *rhubarb* will be among the first to change

Table 4.1 Spelling variants in Internet English

Variant 1	Total (in millions)	Variant 2	Total (in millions)	Ratio
jail	45	gaol	2	22.5:1
encyclopedia	82	encyclopaedia	7	11.7:1
pediatrics	17	paediatrics	2	8.5:1
archaeology	16	archeology	3	5.3:1
aging	48	ageing	10	4.8:1
program	864	programme	184	4.7:1
color	622	colour	148	4.2:1
spelled	14	spelt	4	3.5:1
judgment	57	judgement	19	3:1
jewelry	139	jewellery	48	2.9:1
catalog	388	catalogue	179	2.2:1
analyse	65	analyze	45	1.4:1
yoghurt	21	yogurt	16	1.3:1
disc	148	disk	133	1.1:1
whiskey	15	whisky	14	1.1:1

Table 4.2 Nonstandard spellings in Internet English

Standard spelling	Total (in thousands)	Nonstandard spelling	Total (in thousands)	Ratio (approx.)
building	498,000	bilding	1,830	272:1
guardian	57,700	gardian	334	173:1
handsome	27,500	hansome	255	108:1
autumn	58,200	autum	733	79:1
rhubarb	3,210	rubarb	91	35:1
mnemonic	1,710	nemonic	106	16:1

– in effect, returning to the spelling it had when it first arrived in English. A more learned word, such as *mnemonic*, which has always had an irregular spelling, will be more resistant to change.

GRAMMAR

The distinctiveness of Internet language is found chiefly in graphology and the lexicon – the levels of language where it is relatively easy to introduce innovation and deviation. As with language change in general, grammatical variation is less notice-able. When it does occur on the Internet, it tends to be restricted to a particular situation or group of users, and often gives the impression of being a cult usage. For example, in morphology the old *-en* plural of nouns (found today only in *children*, *oxen*, and *brethren*) has been generalized to a few nouns ending in *-x*, pre-sumably motivated by *vixen*, and seen in such innovative forms as *boxen*, *vaxen* (VAX computers), *matrixen*, and *bixen* (users of the BIX information exchange system). Rather more widely used is the replacement of plural *-s* by *-z* to refer to pirated versions of software, as in *warez*, *tunez*, *gamez*, *serialz*, *pornz*, *downloadz*, and *filez*. But the semantic field is small, and not many lexical items are involved.

Apart from a few cases where computer programmers allow their knowledge of programming syntax to influence the way they write, syntactic constructions on the Internet seem to be the same as those found in non-electronic mediums. There are of course significant differences in sentence length, type, and complexity, related to the constraints of different outputs. The length constraint in texting and tweeting militates against the use of nested subordinate clauses, for example, and a similar propensity to short sentences can be seen in instant messaging and chatroom interaction. But this is not the first time in the history of language that people have used short sentences or avoided elaborate subordination. There is nothing new about the syntactic constructions as such. What we are seeing is the evolution of new styles of discourse (see further p. 75). However, some interesting syntactic developments could be taking place in blogging, which is different from other outputs in that there is no constraint on the length of a post. Some blog posts are thousands of words long, broken down into paragraphs which are themselves of considerable length. Paragraphs are uncommon in forums, and when they do occur they are typically very short. In blogs, they are routine, introduced by writers who are aware that an unbroken mass of text on screen is difficult to read.

It is what happens within the paragraphs that is interesting. This is freely written prose which has not been through the standardizing process normal in all other forms of publicly available literature. Copy-editing procedures ensure that newspapers, magazines, and books conform to an in-house style, and proofreaders are employed to check that the process has been carried out efficiently. It is virtually impossible now to read anything in print which has not been through a standardizing process. But in blogs, we see discourses of sometimes substantial length which have had no such editorial interference. As a consequence, we find syntactic patterns that are never seen in traditional written varieties, other than the occasional literary approximation (such as the stream of consciousness encountered at the end of James Joyce's *Ulysses*). It is a syntax that reflects the way writers think and speak. Linguists know from the analysis of conversation how difficult it is to identify sentence units in informal speech. In blogging, we see the same fluidity of expression taking place in typeset writing.

The discourse expresses a sequence of units of thought which simply do not correspond to the kinds of sentence division we expect to see in print. There is the unconstrained use of the dash to mark a change in the direction of thought, ellipsis dots to show incompleteness, and the use of commas to mark pauses in the rhythm. Here is an extract:

> In the last couple of days I've been blogging away to my heart's content . . . well, as much as my partner will let me, cos we've only got one computer and you wouldn't believe the number of times we both try to use it at the same time – not to mention the power cuts – oh yes, they happen a lot where we live and they're a real pain, but as I say blogging away about – all sorts of things.

This is not the first time people have used such informality in writing: it is a commonplace in informal letters. But it is the first time we have seen such patterns presented in public with the same graphic appearance that we associate with formal print. Some of the sequences defy conventional grammatical analysis in terms of sentence structure. In traditional grammars, much of this kind of writing would have been dismissed as anacoluthon – defined in the *OED* as 'a construction lacking grammatical sequence'. But this misses the point. There *is* grammatical sequence here. The discourse makes perfect sense. It is simply not the same kind of sequence that is recognized in traditional sentence or paragraph analysis. And even linguistically informed grammars would have some difficulty handling material of this kind. This is one of the areas, accordingly, where Internet linguistics can make a contribution to syntactic theory.

PRAGMATICS

Pragmatics studies the choices available to people when they speak or write, and the factors which govern their choice, such as the intention they have in mind or the effect they wish to convey. It was plain very early on in the history of the Internet that the medium was giving rise to types of communication which were unusual by comparison with traditional spoken or written interactions. Pragmatic models of communication, such as the felicity conditions supposed to govern efficient linguistic interaction,[7] do not easily explain the kinds of language seen in some Internet outputs. We find language that offends against the maxim of quality, as when someone sends a message (a *troll*) specifically intended to cause irritation to others, such as the members of a chatgroup. Offences against the maxim of quantity are illustrated by the sending of unwanted information (*spam*) or by spending time in a chatroom without communicating with the other people there (*lurking*). The sending of aggressive or threatening messages (*flaming*) contravenes the maxim of manner. And the presence of random advertisements on a site goes against the maxim of relevance. Why these maxims are flouted is an interesting research question. Anonymity is an important factor: as mentioned in Chapter 1, the Internet is unprecedented in the extent to which people can hide their identity behind nicknames or e-addresses, especially in chatgroups, games, networks, and forums; and when identity is unknown, uninhibited language can result.

A pragmatic perspective is needed in order to analyse the intentions of site-owners and message-senders and to evaluate the effects of their linguistic decisions. For example, what is the illocutionary force of a web page? A page which advertises a particular product is plainly there to produce, in the first instance, an increase in click-through rate, and eventually a sale. What is the perlocutionary effect? Click-through may increase; but if the ad is unintentionally insensitive, a range of unwanted repercussions can appear, such as critical media coverage (for examples, see Chapter 6). This is a clear case. In practice, it is often extremely difficult to say what the intentions are behind a particular web page – or any other kind of Internet activity, for that matter. A web page (or a space within a page) can be used for a range of purposes. It may simply be there to be read as an end in itself – to inform, educate, or entertain. Or its function may be to be acted upon. If the latter, the action may be of several kinds, such as:

- Ask for personally relevant information, as when users need to log in, provide a password, or confirm identity
- Give assistance, as with help buttons, netiquette guidelines, and options to 'contact us'

- Evaluate a product, as with consumer retail reviews
- Obtain feedback about online content, as with forums and comment boxes
- Offer additional functionality, such as related pages ('more like this'), advanced search, bookmarking, or sponsored links
- Enable a purchase, by providing instructions about procedures ('go to basket') and payment methods
- Stop something happening, as with procedures which block pop-up ads or prevent junk mail

In the present state of research, a list of this kind can only be representative, not comprehensive, and the stylistic analysis of the texts relating to each of these categories is in its infancy. Plainly, there is a scale of online adaptability. At one extreme, we find texts where no adaptation to digitally mediated communication has been made – a pdf of an article on screen, for example, with no search or other facilities – in which case, any linguistic analysis would be identical with that of the corresponding offline text. At the other extreme, we find texts which have no counterpart in the offline world. Here are four examples.

Texts whose aim is to defeat spam filters

We only have to look in our email junk folder to discover a world of novel texts whose properties challenge conventional linguistic analysis:

> supr vi-agra online now znwygghsxp
> VI @ GRA 75% off regular xxp wybzz lusfg
> fully stocked online pharmacʌy
> Great deals, prescription d[rugs

It is possible to see a linguistic rationale in the graphological variations in the word *Viagra*, for example, introduced to ensure that it avoids the word-matching function in a filter. We may find the letters spaced (*V i a g r a*), transposed (*Viarga*), duplicated (*Viaggra*), or separated by arbitrary symbols (*Vi*agra*). There are only so many options, and these can to a large extent be predicted (an issue familiar to cryptologists). There is also an anti-linguistic rationale, as one might put it, in which random strings are generated, either of letters (*wybzz*) or words, as in this next example, from a medication supplier:

> pp Center this the century troops in only government the cite years the by and Institute children body species largest p United year that fighter spheres They patron of Slam shores interest Christian Holstein the owned by of The population the fostering when Scandinavia novels and of can the more author Throw population up . . .

These too can be handled, if one's spam filter is linguistically aware, by telling it to remove any message which does not respect the grammatical, punctuational, or graphotactic norms of a language (i.e. the rules governing syllable structure, vowel sequence, or consonant clusters).

Texts whose aim is to guarantee higher rankings in web searches

How is one to ensure that a website appears in the first few hits in a search? There are several techniques, some non-linguistic, some linguistic. An example of a non-linguistic technique is the frequency of hypertext links: the more pages that link to my site, the more likely my page will move up the rankings. An example of a linguistic technique is the listing of key words or phrases which identify the semantic content of a page in the page's metadata: these will be picked up by the search engines and given priority in a search. Neither of these techniques actually alters the linguistic character of the text on a page. Rather different is a third technique, where the text is manipulated to include key words, especially in the heading and first paragraph, to ensure that salient terms are prioritized. The semantic difference can be seen in the following pair of texts (invented, but based on exactly what happens). Text A is an original paragraph; text B is the paragraph rewritten with ranking in mind, to ensure that the product name gets noticed:

A

The Crystal Knitting-Machine is the latest and most exciting product from Crystal Industries. It has an aluminium frame, comes in five exciting colours, and a wide range of accessories.

B

The Crystal Knitting-Machine is the latest and most exciting product from Crystal Industries.

– The Crystal Knitting-Machine has an aluminium frame.
– The Crystal Knitting-Machine comes in five exciting colours.
– The Crystal Knitting-Machine has a wide range of accessories.

Some search engines have now got wise to this technique, and are trying to block it, but it is difficult, in view of the various para-phrases which can be introduced (e.g. *Knitting-Machine from Crystal, Crystal Machines for Knitting*).

Texts whose aim is to save time, energy, or money

Text-messaging is a good example of a text genre whose linguistic characteristics have evolved partly as a response to technological limitations. The limitation to 160 characters (for Roman alpha-bets) has motivated an increased use of nonstandard words (of the *c u l8r* type), using logograms, initialisms, shortenings, and other abbreviatory conventions. The important word is 'partly'. As already discussed in Chapter 1, most of these abbreviations were being used on the Internet long before mobile phones became a routine part of our lives. And the motivation to use them goes well beyond the ergonomic, as their playful character provides entertainment value as an end in itself as well as increas-ing rapport between participants.

Another example of a new type of text arising out of considera-tions of convenience is the email which uses *framing* (mentioned under the heading of 'Persistence' in Chapter 2). We receive a message which contains, say, three different points in a single paragraph. We can, if we want, reply to each of these points by taking the paragraph, splitting it up into three parts, and then responding to each part separately, so that the message we send back then looks a bit like a play dialogue. Then, our sender can do the same thing to our responses, and when we get the message back we see the replies to our replies. We can then send the lot on to someone else for further comments, and when it comes back there are now three voices framed on the screen. And so it can go on – replies within replies within replies – and all unified within the same screen typography. People find this method of response extremely convenient – to an extent, for there comes a point where the nested messages make the text too complex to be easily followed. Research is lacking on the point, but I have never seen an e-exchange which goes beyond six levels of nesting.

Related to framing is intercalated response. Someone sends me a set of questions, or makes a set of critical points about something I have written. I respond to these by intercalating my responses between the points made by the sender. For clarity, I might put my responses in a different colour, or include them in angle brackets or some such convention. A further response from the sender might lead to the use of an additional colour; and if other people are copied in to the exchange, some graphical means of this kind, to distinguish the various participants, is essential.

Texts whose aim is to maintain a standard

Although the Internet is supposedly a medium where freedom of speech is axiomatic, controls and constraints are commonplace to avoid abuses. These range from the excising of obscene and aggressive language to the editing of pages or posts to ensure that they stay focused on a particular topic. Moderators (facilitators, managers, wizards; the terminology is various) have to deal with organizational, social, and content-related issues. When the censoring is carried out automatically, access to innocent pages or messages can be denied if the censoring software is linguistically naive – as has often happened when a potentially sensitive letter sequence (such as *sex*) happens to occur within a broader context (such as *Sussex*). Hundreds of these false positives have been identified in various languages, some of them not easily predictable, as in the case of the software which found the erectile dysfunctional drug *Cialis* in *socialism* and related words. Whether the controls are automated or human, accurate or otherwise, what we end up with is a sanitized text, in which certain parts of language (chiefly vocabulary) are excluded.

STYLES

The Internet has certainly introduced some new linguistic forms into language, ranging from the mildly adaptive (e.g. *tunez*) to the downright bizarre (e.g. *Vi^agr*a*). But only a very small proportion of a language's vocabulary, grammar, and orthography has been affected. For the most part, what we see online looks and sounds very similar to what we see offline. And we would reach the same conclusion if we were to listen to the various auditory resources on the Internet, such as podcasts, 'listen again' radio features, and Skype conversations. The occasional new form is striking and may be frequent (as in the use of *tube* and *youtube* as verbs in YouTube speech and captions: *Wanna know where I tube? I tube/youtube from Rome*[8]), but most of the linguistic forms encountered will be familiar. The main evidence for language change on the Internet is not to be found here, but rather in the discourse patterns that characterize the various outputs.

It is useful, in this connection, to see the Internet in relation to what has happened during previous advances in communication technology. On each occasion there has been the emergence of novel language management strategies. Printing introduced such features as page numbering, content summaries, headlines, and indexes. The telephone required conventional expressions of identification and greeting. Broadcasting promoted the choice of a nationally intelligible accent and dialect, along with decisions about which pronunciation to use when usage was divided. The language associated with each technology was mediated by new kinds of professional, such as typesetters, copy-editors, proof-readers, telephone operators, and radio announcers. The outcome was the emergence of situationally distinctive uses of language (*varieties*, as I have been calling them) associated with each technology.

As each technology became established, different types of product appeared. Printing gave rise to the different kinds of publication, such as books, pamphlets, newspapers, magazines, posters, calendars, and brochures. Radio gave rise to the various programmes and presentation routines, as encountered in newsreading, announcing, weather forecasting, sports commentary, and commercial breaks. Each of these products became associated with a particular kind of language, identifiable with reference to particular features of phonology, graphology, grammar, vocabulary, and discourse. Studies appeared with such titles as 'The language of advertising' and 'The language of news reporting', and the analysis of varieties became the chief focus of the branch of linguistics known as general (as opposed to literary) stylistics.[9] Today, a stylistic analysis of a variety is a complex business, especially in cases where the content of the output is diverse. A newspaper, for example, is a composite containing several varieties of language – reports, editorials, opinion pieces, information summaries, cartoons, word games, advertisements, and more. In some cases, it is possible to see varieties operating at different levels of generality: the variety of sports commentary, for example, can be seen as consisting of several 'sub-varieties' associated with individual sports.

The new varieties of language resulting from each technological innovation have always added to whatever existed before. When the production of manuscripts for public consumption was replaced by printing, handwriting did not disappear; handwritten texts continued to be used in such situations as personal tuition, creative writing, and private correspondence. When telephones were invented, the new techniques of voice-to-voice (as opposed to face-to-face) communication did not change the way people talked to each other in the street. People did not start speaking like sports commentators or newsreaders after encountering these genres on the radio. Nor did the distinctive style of some forms of journalism ('Said 33-year-old mother-of-two Jane . . .') cause people to alter their personal writing preferences. Rather, in each case we see new varieties being added to those already there. New technologies always increase a language's stylistic range.

The same process has happened with the Internet. The various kinds of online activity have resulted in novel language management strategies, such as domain names, URLs, file archives, identity profiles, security measures, and spam filters. New intermediaries have appeared, such as web designers, developers, and administrators, and the various species of moderator who monitor chatrooms, bulletin boards, and online games. And, as electronic technology has evolved, so we have seen a diverse set of outputs, such as email, chat, gaming, the web, instant messaging, blogging, social networking, texting, and tweeting. The recency of electronically mediated communication, and the speed at which it is changing (as illustrated in Chapter 1), means that we cannot specify the linguistic features of each output with the same confidence or depth of detail as we would be able to do with, say, scientific language or sports commentary. But, at a general level, the situational constraints needed to differentiate varieties are clearly present on the Internet, reflected in the kinds of screen structure and functionality which the software makes available to the user. Examples are the various structural elements of blogs (posts, links, comments, etc.), the expressive limits of texts (160 characters) and tweets (140 characters), and the hypertextuality and graphic richness of web pages.

The stylistic analysis of Internet language has hardly begun, and in some cases the outputs are so recent that it is unclear at what level the notion of variety best applies. The constraints operating on Twitter, for example, are such that it is likely to present a fairly homogeneous linguistic character, so the notion of variety will readily apply. By contrast, the web is stylistically so diverse that it makes little sense to talk about 'the language of the web' at all. In between, there are outputs whose stylistic status is unclear. Is there a single variety of social networking, with the different companies (Facebook, LinkedIn, Bebo, MySpace, etc.) demonstrating 'sub-varieties', or are the differences in functionality so great that we would wish to call them varieties in their own right? It is an empirical question, awaiting the description of the linguistic properties of each, but, as there are over 170 such companies active (in 2011), the task facing linguists is considerable.

See also 'Research directions and activities', pp. 154–5.

5

A MULTILINGUAL INTERNET

The Internet may as yet have had only a limited role in fostering language change, but it has already played a major role in fostering language presence. This has been the most notable development within the medium since the 1990s, and one which seems set to continue. The Internet offers a home to all languages – as soon as their communities have an electricity supply and a functioning computer technology. Its increasingly multilingual character has been the most notable change since its beginnings as a totally English medium. There is a story told from that decade by the former US vice-president Al Gore. He was reporting the remark of the 8-year-old son of Kyrgyzstan's President Akayev, who told his father that he had to learn English. When asked why, the child apparently replied: 'Because the computer speaks English.'

For some time, indeed, there was a widespread impression that English was the language of the Internet. A headline in the *New York Times* in 1996 said simply: 'World, Wide, Web: 3 English Words'. The article, by Michael Specter, went on to say: 'if you want to take full advantage of the Internet there is only one real way to do it: learn English'. He did acknowledge the arrival of other languages: 'As the Web grows, the number of people on it who speak French, say, or Russian will become more varied and that variety will be expressed on the Web. That is why it is a fundamentally democratic technology' – adding 'but it won't necessarily happen soon'.[1]

It is now clear that this conclusion was wrong. Since the mid-1990s, the presence of other languages has steadily risen. A widely quoted figure of the time was that about 80 per cent of the Internet was in English – though such figures always have to be treated cautiously, as much depends on what exactly is being counted (users, pages, sites, hosts . . .) and methodological issues abound (see further p. 86). In 2001, the US Internet Council reported that English had lost its dominance, represented by 45 per cent of the online population.[2] Table 5.1 is a typical illustration of the change in direction, showing the top ten Internet languages at the beginning of 2010 in terms of number of users. English continues to hold the leading position, but is likely to be soon replaced by Chinese, a language which has been increasing its Internet presence over four times more quickly than English during the first decade of the millennium (see Column 5). Internet penetration (Column 4) is the percentage of the speakers of a language thought to be using the Internet. The figure for Chinese is

Table 5.1 Top ten Internet languages, measured by users, in 2010

Languages	Percentage of all Internet users	Internet users (in millions)	Percentage Internet penetration	Percentage Internet language growth (2000–09)
English	27.5	496	39.4	252
Chinese	22.6	408	29.7	1,162
Spanish	7.8	140	34.0	669
Japanese	5.3	96	75.5	104
Portuguese	4.3	78	31.4	924
German	4.0	72	75.0	161
Arabic	3.3	60	17.5	2,298
French	3.2	57	16.9	375
Russian	2.5	45	32.3	1,360
Korean	2.1	37	52.7	97
Others	17.4	314	13.3	516
World total	100.0	1,802	26.6	399

relatively low, compared with English, but this situation could quickly change.

A related question is which parts of the world have the greatest potential for increasing the multilingual character of the Internet. Table 5.2 summarizes the situation at the level of continents. The greatest area of language growth is in Africa, which has the lowest level of Internet penetration. As Africa is home to around a third of the world's languages, it is obvious that, as its online presence grows, it will have a significant impact on the multilingual character of the Internet. However, for this to happen there will need to be a considerable development in supporting infrastructure. At present, reliable electricity reaches only some 5 per cent of the population, and the percentage of fixed telephone lines is the lowest worldwide, averaging (in 2007) four lines for 100 people.[3] This seriously constrains the deployment of broadband access with ADSL (the method used in most countries), which reaches above 1 per cent in only a few areas. There are also many hidden costs involved, such as the persistent need to upgrade software and hardware, and the provision of adequate technological support, which places an easy-to-use Internet beyond the reach of poorer nations. It is significant that nearly 90 per cent of the global IT market belongs to the G7 group of countries: Canada, France, Germany, Italy, Japan, UK, USA.[4]

Table 5.2 World Internet use

Areas	Internet users (in millions)	Percentage Internet penetration	Percentage Internet growth (2000–09)
Africa	86	9	1,810
Middle East	58	29	1,675
Central America	34	23	975
South America	143	36	901
Asia	764	20	569
Europe	426	53	305
Oceania	21	61	177
Caribbean	9	23	155
North America	260	76	140

On the other hand, all 54 countries and territories in Africa do now have Internet access in their main cities, and there has been significant recent growth. At the beginning of 2008 only 4.7 per cent of the people had access to the Internet. By the beginning of 2010, the penetration had risen to 8.7 per cent, as shown in Table 5.2. The growth was over 1,809 per cent between 2000 and 2009. Even more important is the fact that Africa has 280 million telephone subscribers, 65 per cent of whom are mobile subscribers – the highest ratio of mobile to total telephone subscribers of any region in the world. Africa is also the region with the highest mobile growth rate, averaging around 65 per cent per year in the mid-2000s. With access to the Internet via mobile phones being one of the major growth areas, this could greatly alter the African Internet linguistic scenario. It should also be noted that growing numbers of Africans access the Internet not through personal subscriptions but through Internet cafes. Under such circumstances, with a growing audience and demand, we might expect the Internet – as has happened elsewhere – to increasingly reflect an African linguistic demographic.

The demand is certainly there, and not only in Africa. All else being equal, people like to read, write, listen, and speak on the Internet in their first language. As early as 2001, surveys such as those provided by the Interactive Data Corporation[5] were reporting significant Internet preferences for own-language use – 62 per cent in France, 79 per cent in Germany, 84 per cent in Japan, 85 per cent in China. Figures of this order of magnitude remain robust, even after allowing for an increase in English-language use by the various countries, because they reflect preferences, not abilities. Customers were said to be four times more likely to buy if approached in their own language. And the economic argument for Internet multilingualism was repeatedly heard in subsequent years.

However, the critical phrase is 'all else being equal'. When we examine the Internet to establish the range and quality of content, we find huge disparities across languages. Languages are patently not equal. The Internet is dominated by a small number of languages – just ten of them occupy over 80 per cent of Internet space (Table 5.1). Nobody has yet worked out how many languages have a presence on the Internet, or how much content is associated with them.[6] But it is clear, for many languages, that the amount of data is quite small and often specialized, and sometimes has little more than a symbolic role. One site has resources in 728 languages, but the focus is on e-commerce. Another claims to have recordings of over 5,800 languages or dialects, but the content is largely restricted to retellings of the Bible story.[7] Even when an entire site operates in more than one language, there may not be complete localization – for example, it may not be able to take payments in local currency, or its helpline may be available only through a foreign network. The Internet will one day represent the distribution of language presence in the world, but it is currently a long way from that ideal. For a multilingual Internet to grow, there has to be policy agreement and technological implementation, and such things take time to put in place.

POLICY AND TECHNOLOGY

At a policy level, there have been several statements and resolutions affirming the desirability of a multilingual Internet. The first major step was in October 2003, during the thirty-second session of UNESCO's General Conference. That is the meeting where UNESCO adopted the convention on the preservation of the world's intangible heritage (including endangered languages); but at the same meeting it also made a set of recommendations concerning the promotion and use of multilingualism and access to cyberspace. The first five recommendations were all statements of strong support for the online development of multilingualism, and they are worth quoting in full:[8]

1.   The public and private sectors and the civil society at local, national, regional and international levels should work to provide the necessary resources and take the necessary measures to alleviate language barriers and promote human interaction on the Internet by encouraging the creation and processing of, and access to, educational, cultural and scientific content in digital form, so as to ensure that all cultures

can express themselves and have access to cyberspace in all languages, including indigenous ones.

2. Member States and international organizations should encourage and support capacity-building for the production of local and indigenous content on the Internet.

3. Member States should formulate appropriate national policies on the crucial issue of language survival in cyberspace, designed to promote the teaching of languages, including mother tongues, in cyberspace. International support and assistance to developing countries should be strengthened and extended to facilitate the development of freely accessible materials on language education in electronic form and to the enhancement of human capital skills in this area.

4. Member States, international organizations and information and communication technology industries should encourage collaborative participatory research and development on, and local adaptation of, operating systems, search engines and web browsers with extensive multilingual capabilities, online dictionaries and terminologies. They should support international cooperative efforts with regard to automated translation services accessible to all, as well as intelligent linguistic systems such as those performing multilingual information retrieval, summarizing/abstracting and speech understanding, while fully respecting the right of translation of authors.

5. UNESCO, in cooperation with other international organizations, should establish a collaborative online observatory on existing policies, regulations, technical recommendations, and best practices relating to multilingualism and multilingual resources and applications, including innovations in language computerization.

Following these guidelines, the first phase of the World Summit on the Information Society quickly followed in Geneva (December 2003), with a second phase in Tunis (November 2005). The outcome was a commitment to work towards the multilingualization of the Internet involving all stakeholders, including governments. Three Action Lines were identified: the International

Telecommunications Union (ITU) would take the lead role in the implementation of information and communication infrastructure; ITU and UNESCO together would look after access to information and knowledge; and UNESCO would take responsibility for cultural diversity and identity, linguistic diversity and local content. The ITU and UNESCO then held a global symposium on promoting the multilingual Internet in Geneva (May 2006). A plenipotentiary conference of the ITU in Antalya, Turkey (November 2006) affirmed the need to make Internet content available in non-Roman-based scripts. The following year, the ITU and UNESCO, along with the Internet Corporation for Assigned Names and Numbers (ICANN) – the organization which since 1998 has coordinated the Internet's naming system – held a workshop in Rio de Janeiro (November 2007) on global progress in forging universal standards needed in a multilingual cyberspace.

A great deal of cyberpolicy, then, was in place early on, but it took some time before this began to be translated into cyberreality. A critical step was the need to enable non-Roman writing systems to be domain names. As early as 2003 a mechanism was defined for handling names containing non-ASCII characters: it was called Internationalizing Domain Names in Applications (IDNA). Tests began on implementing the system, but it took five years before it was finally approved, and it was only in 2009 that ICANN announced the creation of country-code top-level domains – a development that ICANN president Rod Beckstrom described at the time as 'truly momentous'. As he put it at the ICANN Board Meeting of 30 October:[9]

> this represents today one small step for ICANN . . . but it represents a very important and significant step for half the world of Internet users. Those who use non-Latin scripts and their own language.

It was only a first step. The decision was only for country-code domains, not for other domain names, such as .org and .net. But it was a significant development, and recognized as such, greeted with a standing ovation at the ICANN meeting. Several countries immediately applied, with Arabic, Russian, and Chinese implementations introduced in mid-2010.

Until quite recently there were real problems in using the characters of the keyboard to cope with the alphabetical diversity of the world's languages. Because the English alphabet was the standard, only a very few non-English accents and diacritics could be handled. If it was a foreign word with some strange-looking accent marks, the Internet software would simply ignore them, and assume they weren't important. This can still happen – but things have moved on a great deal. First, the basic set of keyboard characters, the so-called ASCII set, was extended, so that the commoner non-English diacritics could be included. But even then it only allowed up to 256 characters. After several years of preliminary planning, the Unicode Consortium was formed in 1991, with the aim of providing a universal character encoding platform. Unicode encodes characters that appear in a script, regardless of the number of languages that might use it. From this point of view, a script which is used for a single language is just as important as one that is used for several hundred. All scripts are indeed equal. The first version was released in June 1993, and by October 2009 had reached version 5.2, which supports 90 scripts (see Table 5.3) and 107,156 linguistic symbols, along with a range of other graphs, such as punctuation marks, numerals, Braille, mathematical symbols, and phonetic symbols.[10]

The situation is steadily becoming increasingly promising for minority and endangered languages. The Internet is, after all, the ideal medium for such languages. If you are a speaker or supporter of an endangered language – an aboriginal language, say, or a language like Welsh or Basque – you are keen to give the language some publicity, to draw its situation to the attention of the world. Previously, it was not easy. It was difficult to attract the interest of a newspaper or a broadcasting station, and purchasing space in publications was expensive. But now, with web pages waiting to be used, and email there at the cost of a phone call, you can get your message out in next to no time, in your own language – with a translation as well, if you want – and in front of a global audience whose potential size makes traditional media audiences look minuscule by comparison.

There is a second reason, relating to the question of how one maintains a minority or endangered language. Teenagers play a

Table 5.3 Scripts encoded in Unicode 5.2

Europe	Armenian, Coptic, Cypriot Syllabary, Cyrillic, Georgian, Glagolithic, Gothic, Greek, Latin, Linear B, Ogham, Old Italic, Phaistos Disc, Runic, Shavian
Africa	Bamum, Egyptian hieroglyphs, Ethiopic, N'Ko, Osmanya, Tifinagh, Vai
Middle East	Arabic, Aramaic, Avestan, Carian, Cuneiform, Hebrew, Lycian, Lydian, Old South Arabian, Pahlavi, Parthian, Phoenician, Samaritan, Syriac
Central Asia	Mongolian, Old Turkic, Phags-Pa, Tibetan
South Asia	Bengali, Devanagari, Gujarati, Gurmukhi, Kaithi, Kannada, Kharoshthi, Lepcha, Limbu, Malayalam, Meetei Mayek, Ol Chiki, Oriya, Saurashtra, Sinhala, Syloti Nagri, Tamil, Telugu, Thaana, Vedic
South-East Asia	Balinese, Buginese, Cham, Javanese, Kayah Li, Khmer, Lao, Myanmar, New Tai Lue, Rejang, Sundanese, Tai Le, Tai Tham, Tai Viet, Thai
Philippines	Bhid, Hanunoo, Tagalog, Tagbanwa
East Asia	Bopomofo, Chinese ideographs, Hangul, Hiragana, Kanbun, Katakana, Lisu, Yi
America	Canadian Aboriginal, Cherokee, Deseret

critical role, as they are the parents of the next generation of children, and if their enthusiasm for their ancestral language wanes the outlook is unpromising. The task, then, is to provide teenagers with the opportunity to use their ancestral language in motivating situations, and here the Internet is central (at least, so far, for those languages that have developed a written form), for few things motivate teenagers more than electronically mediated communication. The task is not easy, given the huge amount of enticing online content in the majority languages where they live, which cannot be disregarded; but progress has been made in several communities, where online bilingual chatrooms, forums, and social networking sites offer a platform to all the languages encountered in the social milieu of the participants.[11]

METHODOLOGICAL ISSUES

Industry surveys of language diversity on the Internet have been carried out by a number of organizations, and are widely reported. All, however, have to be treated with extreme caution, as their procedures differ. Very different results would be obtained if an analyst counted users, web pages, websites, or host servers. The amount of language represented on a website also varies, ranging from total translation to a token presence. An important task of Internet linguistics is to evaluate the claims about language use that have been made and to develop more reliable quantitative measures. Peter Gerrand, for example, has made a series of important distinctions, recapitulated in the following paragraphs.[12]

It is possible to count the number of active Internet users in a country, and establish *user profiles*, but there is no easy way to determine the language they actually use from such statistics. Industry surveys make a number of questionable assumptions, such as that online use will have a direct relationship to offline use. If 20 per cent of the population of Wales speak Welsh, then (it is implied) 20 per cent will use Welsh on the Internet. This is far from being the case, for a variety of reasons. Welsh speakers do not all have Internet access at home. Not everyone able to speak Welsh is equally able (or willing) to read and write in it. People display differential language skills, especially when there is a choice to be made between a dominant and minority language. And even when these factors do not apply, the decision whether to use Welsh or English is very much dependent on sociolinguistic and stylistic factors. A user might find Welsh appropriate for everyday chat but not for business communication, or vice versa. Just because people speak a language at home does not mean they will automatically use that language when they type (or speak) on the Internet.

The assumption of offline/online equivalence becomes even more suspect when we consider communities where choices have to be made between several languages, such as French, German, Romansch, and English in Switzerland. The likelihood is that minority languages will have their Internet use overestimated, and majority languages will have it underestimated. In particular, international languages will be seriously underestimated, which is why we need to be cautious about accepting the general view that the use of English on the Internet is significantly declining.

At best, user profiles show the *potential* use of a language. They are helpful for policy makers who wish to promote a particular language on the Internet, but they do not provide a reliable guide to active language use.

Measures of *user activity* are far more useful, as these aim to plot the actual use of a language on the Internet, using outputs where contributions can be clearly identified, such as posts to a forum or a chatroom. In principle we can take a sample of Internet traffic and quantify the use of individual languages within it. However, for this to be done for large samples, a reliable language identifying system has to be deployed automatically, and this is not quite as easy to provide as might at first appear. Researchers immediately come up against the issue of accessibility, especially in the case of outputs (such as email, chat, instant messaging, and voice-over-Internet) where questions of privacy and ownership are critical. But even when this issue is overcome, there are linguistic problems to be solved.

To ensure that most posts in a particular language are identified, especially when they are short (as with Twitter), the system has to make use of key words or phrases that are most likely to appear. The problem is that high-frequency words are often short and linguistically ambiguous. *Le*, for example, could be a word in French, Italian, Spanish, or several other languages. To ensure that a language filter is effective, several hundred items thus have to be included – a figure that increases significantly in highly inflected languages, where several variant forms of a lexeme are encountered. The ideal method would be to match the words in a post against an entire dictionary of a language, with inflections expanded, but when billions of posts have to be analysed in this way a huge amount of processing power is involved. (A similar problem arises in relation to the processing of ad impressions, p. 117.) Processing spoken material raises additional problems of speech recognition.

Most estimates of Internet language presence have been based on counting pages present on the web – these days, using the mechanisms provided by the various search engines – but here too there are several difficulties to be overcome. To begin with, the engines vary enormously in their databases and mechanisms, so that a search can yield very different results – as can be quickly shown by looking for an individual word (see further, p. 141). A search for *laboratoire* using Google resulted in 156 million hits, whereas on AltaVista the total was 56 million, and these results vary further depending on which language filters are used in the search (all languages vs French alone). These totals are in any case approximate because they conflate pages from different times (p. 31), rely on sources of data from different times (population census data can be ten or more years old), and contain an unknown number of duplicated pages. As Gerrand puts it:

> The variation is so great across page counts for the same word and same language choice that one can have no confidence that these three search engines have crawled the same parts of the web. Nor can one have confidence that any of them have crawled over more than a fraction of the public web.

These problems are exacerbated by the linguistic limitations of search engines. Languages are not treated equally, because of limitations in the technology. Those which use non-Roman scripts, in particular, may not be readily available on a home computer, so that people are predisposed to use other languages.

A related problem is that some industry surveys rely uncritically on the data provided by the available sources of demographic linguistic data, notably Ethnologue. While everyone appreciates the amount of detailed work that has gone into this remarkable project since its inception in 1951, its limited resources inevitably mean that reported data varies in quality. In a report submitted in 2006 to the UNESCO Institute of Statistics, John Paolillo and Anupam Das took a random sample of 2001 entries for population data from the 2005 edition and found that a surprising 52.4 per cent had sources before 1996; moreover, 2.1 per cent dated from between 1975 and as far back as 1920.[13] Here are some specific examples, using data from their paper and also from Gerrand (2007).

The 2005 edition showed 28.2 million first-language Spanish speakers in Spain, based on the 1986 census. As there was a census in 2001 in Spain, we might expect a considerable increase in both these totals. For Spain's regional languages, data on

Catalan was from 1996, Basque from 1991, and Galician from 1986. English was no better treated. Ethnologue 2005 still gave totals for native English speakers from 1984 for the USA and UK, 1987 for Australia and New Zealand, 1996 for South Africa, and 1998 for Canada. Its estimate of 11 million second-language English speakers in India was based on India's 1961 census; the real total is probably around 300 million, though it all depends on the levels of fluency recognized. The dates tend not to be mentioned when such figures are quoted on the Internet. People cite Ethnologue assuming that all the figures are equal, when in fact they are highly asynchronic.

When it comes to the information about languages available on the web, the situation is just as unsatisfactory. UNESCO has noticed the point. In January 2006, the Communications and Information Sector's *In Focus* web column asked the rhetorical question: 'Is it reasonable to define and direct linguistic policies in digital space without having sufficient, accurate, and precise indicators on the situation of languages and their progress?'[14] It asked for an academic response, and in 2007 Gerrand provided one, identifying a methodology which would introduce a level of consistency into web reports. In a letter to Riek Smeets in September 2007 he suggested 'that UNESCO co-ordinate the development of databases of readily accessible, online statistics on use of the world's written languages on the Internet (i.e. their web presence), as well as reasonably up-to-date online statistics on the world's spoken language populations (i.e. user profiles)'.[15] The task is difficult, for other associated factors need to be addressed before we can achieve the desired level of consistency – such as better census data. Very few countries actually collect census data on the languages spoken within their territory. When they do, it is often not easy to find. And those that do, do not ask the same questions. They vary in the attention they pay to speaking, listening, reading, writing, and signing. They vary in their reference to first and other languages. They vary in the way in which questions are phrased, e.g. positively (*Which languages do you understand?*) or negatively (*Which languages don't you understand?*). But these are nettles which have to be grasped, if the situation is to improve.

So, we continue to use the statistics provided by industry surveys because there is nothing better; but it would be naive to quote claims about frequency of language use out of context. It is essential to know what was counted, how it was counted, and when it was counted. We also need to know which outputs were taken into account – websites, email, blogs, etc. – for the results are likely to vary. There is no doubt that the Internet is steadily becoming increasingly multilingual, but it will be some time before we can achieve a sophisticated understanding of what this actually means.

See also 'Research directions and activities', pp. 155–8.

6

APPLIED INTERNET LINGUISTICS

Applied linguistics is the application of linguistic theories, models, methods, concepts, and research findings to the elucidation and solution of problems in fields where language plays a central role. The Internet is such a field, as it is totally dependent on language, whether written or spoken. Even in cases of websites which on screen seem to consist of no more than images, language is present in the underlying content specification of the pages (part of the *metadata*); and until such time as advanced visual pattern-recognition techniques are developed, it is not possible for such pages to be found and indexed without linguistic support. Problems of Internet management are therefore likely to need investigation using the same kind of perspective that has proved to be successful in such other domains of applied linguistics as foreign language teaching, forensic science, and speech pathology.

It is not possible to provide a review of the many Internet-related projects that have begun to use insights from linguistics in recent years, because much of the information is unavailable. This is a fiercely competitive field, and companies which have invested heavily in developing a particular application are naturally unwilling to expose their methods to competitive risk. I am in the same position, having worked on particular products for a series of Internet companies since the mid-1990s.[1] I can use this experience to illustrate the general linguistic issues involved, but I am unable to go into detail about the proposed solutions. Linguists who wish to get involved in this burgeoning field will encounter similar constraints if they collaborate with an Internet company. They may have to sign non-disclosure agreements and understand that they do not necessarily own the results of their research. Students who have a doctoral thesis in mind, or academics who wish to write a book, must therefore make every effort to discuss with the company in advance what they will be permitted to achieve. It is not the first time that applied linguists have found themselves in this position (there are precedents in forensic linguistics and lexicography, for example), but in the world of the Internet the stakes are much higher.

PROBLEM AREAS

The first step, in any applied linguistic enquiry, is to define the problems in need of solution. In the context of the Internet, these are diverse, depending on the area of online activity, and can be illustrated from several fields. Each field presents difficulties arising out of the lack of a linguistically sophisticated frame of reference.

Search engine assistance

With search engines, the requirement is to receive accurate, relevant, and up-to-date hits. It is a common experience that this requirement is not met. A request from a search engine for information about *apples* (where the enquirer had in mind the fruit) produced several million hits, but all the results on the opening page were about computers and the Beatles, including several results which were seriously out of date. An economist who typed in *depression*, expecting information about the financial climate, was swamped with results to do with mental health. Improving the relevance, accuracy, and up-to-dateness of search queries, without making the user do all the work (e.g. by adding extra search words or scrolling through pages of hits), is a continual goal of search engine companies, especially those trying to compete with Google. From the enquirer's point of view, the aim is to save time and obtain the most meaningful hits. From a website-owner's point of view, the aim is to achieve a high ranking for the site in any set of results.

Plainly the problems arise from the polysemic character of the words. The various senses of a word (*apple*, *depression*) are not being distinguished. In the case of *depression*, there has been a failure to separate the senses relating to the knowledge categories of mental health, meteorology, economics, and geology. It might be thought that simply increasing the number of search terms will improve the relevance of hits in relation to enquiries: this turns out to be not always the case. If we choose exactly the right additional words, we may indeed get more relevant results. But it is by no means easy deciding what those additional words should be. If we do not choose well, the expanded query can result in a collection of results which are even more diverse than the original single-word query. The reason is that it is not the number of extra query terms which makes a good search, but the number of extra terms *in context*. If we are interested in the electrical sense of *charge*, adding *power* would not necessarily give us an unambiguous result, because there are too many sites where *charge* and *power* go together in the context of military science, economics, and other domains. A semantic perspective is essential.

Document classification

In automatic document classification, the requirement is to find all files which deal with a specific topic or combination of topics. Failure here can be illustrated from a law-firm where a solicitor was unable to find all the documents in a database relating to a case in Bosnia and Herzegovina because he searched only for the name of the country in that orthographic form and did not search for *Bosnia-Herzegovina*, *Bosnia & Herzegovina* and other alternatives. Another found himself flooded with unwanted documents because a search for *New Mexico* also brought in material from Mexico, New York, and other locations containing the word *New*. In the first case, important information relating to the precedents in a case was not retrieved. In the second, much time was wasted, as the lawyers had to read through a great deal of material before discovering that a document was irrelevant.

Here we see the ambiguity problem in relation to place names. A glance at any gazetteer will show that the same name (*Lancaster*, *Newtown*) can turn up dozens of times in various countries. The orthographic variation encountered in the Bosnia example is just one variable, made more difficult when accents (often ignored by the software) are part of the words. Not all searches can be made successful by the simple expedient of adding an extra locator (e.g. *Lancaster* + *UK*). For example, it is not a straightforward matter to frame a search so that it finds only entries on the state of *New Mexico* while ignoring all entries relating to the country of *Mexico*. Here too, a semantic perspective is essential, with multi-word place names also raising issues of grammatical analysis and graphology.

E-commerce

In e-commerce, the requirement is to enable users to obtain data quickly and accurately about specific products in online catalogues. Again, there are many instances where this requirement is not met. In one online retail site, an enquiry for 'shampoo' (where the enquirer meant 'hair shampoo') received a cluster of responses mainly about carpet shampoo and car shampoo. Disentangling these proved frustrating and time-consuming. Another, to an online bookstore, asked for books by 'David Crystal'; among the list of books received were some by the linguist and some by a Scottish poet with the same name. There was no way of determining which book belonged to which author. The confusion was compounded by the 'further information' provided: 'people who bought this book', said the text accompanying a book written by the Scottish poet, 'also bought the following . . .' – listing several books by linguists. With a really common name, such as various writers called John Smith, the possibilities for confusion are legion.

The retail industry is keen to develop more customer-friendly methods of interrogating online databases, but finds it difficult to anticipate all the factors which impede good communication. An example is the inadequate specification of variant forms. A search for *mobile phones* on an electronic equipment retail site received the implausible response: 'we have no mobile phones'. Repeated attempts using various lexical, grammatical, and orthographic variants (e.g. *mobile-phone*, *mobile phones*, *cellphones*, *cellphones*) all received the same negative response. Eventually it transpired that the only search term the software recognized was *cellular phones*. Faced with such e-uncooperativeness, many people would not have the patience to continue their enquiry, and sales could be lost.

Why did the problem arise? The various contexts in which the word *shampoo* appears were not distinguished because the enquirer had not anticipated the ambiguity by using a more specific search term. In this example, the alternatives are easy to see, as *shampoo* is a concrete term with few senses. In the case of words which have many senses, or which are more abstract in meaning, such as *depression*, it is not always obvious how to express a search in such a way that all the unwanted contexts are excluded. In the case of the Amazon authors, the problem arose because of the lack of an appropriate authorial classification in terms of either biography or subject-matter. In the *mobile phones* example, the factors being ignored were to do with British and American English, grammatical number, and orthographic conventions.

Online advertising

In online advertising, there is a primary requirement to ensure that ads which appear on a website are relevant, focused, and sensitive to the content of a page. However, there are thousands of instances every day where this requirement is not met. We call up a football site and the ads on the page suggest we buy chocolate or bicycles – but not sportswear or footballs. We enter a social networking forum about cars, and the banner ad offers us cameras or gardening equipment – but not good deals on cars or garages or motoring organizations. Even after more than a decade of Internet evolution, inappropriate ad placement on sites and pages is a frequent daily occurrence. Here are some more examples from my own collection (taken from various countries):

- Advertising for a shot put alongside a story of a helicopter shot down in Iraq.
- Advertising for Trojan condoms alongside a review of the movie *Troy*.
- Advertising for a DIY garden bridge alongside a description of the card game.
- Advertising for a French TV company (Canal Plus) alongside a site about the Panama Canal.

The ads are irrelevant to the content of the page, and a marketing opportunity has been missed.

A rather different kind of inappropriate placement is illustrated by these examples:

- Advertising kitchen knives alongside a news report about a stabbing.
- Advertising trips to a country alongside a news item reporting rebel fighting in that country.
- Advertising cheap airline flights alongside a news report of a plane crash.
- Advertising a film alongside a review which says the film is terrible.
- Advertising cheap gas alongside a site about tours of Auschwitz.

Here the ads are insensitive and embarrassing rather than irrelevant – and in some cases horribly so. The advertising industry is keen to develop more sophisticated methods of targeting ads on pages in order to guarantee relevance and avoid insensitive misplacement. Companies are naturally upset when their ad agency places their products on irrelevant pages or in embarrassing locations. It harms their image and loses them sales.

Once again, the problem can be simply diagnosed. In the *stabbing* example, the software has found the word *knife* appearing several times in the news report, assumed that this was what the page is about, and looked for the same word in the available ad inventory. It has ignored the fact that *knife* = 'weapon' and *knife* = 'cutlery' are very different linguistic entities. A similar ambiguity lies behind all the other examples: *gas* = 'method of killing' is not the same as *gas* = 'source of domestic energy'.

THE FOCUS ON AMBIGUITY

The above examples suggest a clear direction for linguistic research. There is a common underlying theme: the Internet situations do not take sufficiently into account the ambiguity inherent in the use of language. The problems that face anyone trying to carry out online searching can be summed up in three words: irrelevance, incoherence, and inaccuracy. And underneath all of these lies polysemy – the fact that words (more technically, *lexical items* or *lexemes*) in a language typically have more than one meaning, and thus present a permanent potential ambiguity. The point is a truism among linguists, but it is much less appreciated in the Internet industry, which often operates as if ambiguity did not exist. An important aspect of applied Internet linguistics, therefore, is to provide the industry with a more sophisticated linguistic perspective.

There are two ways of resolving ambiguity, grammatical and lexical, and both have potential for application. This can be illustrated from any ambiguous word, such as *charge*. Seen in isolation, it is impossible to say what this word means. It is not that it has no meaning; rather it has too much meaning, in that it contains several competing senses – military, electrical, legal, monetary, etc. – only one of which (leaving puns aside) will be relevant to a particular context. To find the relevant sense, we can adopt a grammatical approach, using the word within a sentence, where the various sentence elements (such as type of subject, object, or adverbial) combine to help 'select' the required meaning:

I ordered the troops to charge.
I need to charge the battery.
I'm going to charge him with an offence.
The bank want to charge extra interest.

We can also provide information about word-class – such as whether the word is functioning as a noun, verb, or adjective, or a particular subclass (such as countable or uncountable noun, transitive or intransitive verb):

We make a charge for delivery.
They charge you for delivery.
I have a charge card with me.

A full parse of a sentence, taking account of its formal and functional properties, is an important procedure in helping to resolve ambiguity, and is at the core of a great deal of work in computational linguistics.

In a lexical approach to the problem, a set of associated words (*collocations*) is specified without providing any grammatical context. The various senses are distinguished by connecting a word to other words with which it has strong linguistic associations:

charge – army, commander, order . . .
charge – electricity, cable, battery . . .
charge – crime, police, serious . . .
charge – interest, cost, pay . . .

Not all collocations make good discriminators. *Power*, for example, would not be a good way of distinguishing the military and the electrical senses. *Amount* would not distinguish the economic and electrical senses. It takes a careful analysis to work out which words can act as discriminators in this way and which cannot, and to establish which collocations are 'key', for a particular word. But both these tasks have to be done, if we want to make sense of search from a lexical point of view.

A combination of grammatical and lexical perspectives is likely to provide the best results in solving problems of ambiguity.

In practice, projects have begun from one or other of these positions. In my own work, the problem of deciding between competing syntactic models, along with the lack of reference grammars providing analyses at the required depth of detail for different languages, led me to look for a lexical solution, where appropriate resources in the form of dictionaries and encyclopedias (see further p. 103) were readily available. Applied linguists, faced with demands from an industry or profession which wants results as soon as possible, often find themselves in the position of opting for an approach which will achieve reasonable results relatively quickly, while knowing that a more powerful solution is likely in the long term.

It is important, in any Internet project, to get a sense of the scale of a problem. Just how much polysemy is there in a language? If we take a concise or college dictionary, such as the *Concise Oxford* or the *Webster New Collegiate* – usually containing 1,500 to 2,000 pages – we will find that it contains around 100,000 headwords. It is difficult to be precise, because dictionaries count headwords in different ways. One dictionary counts *nation, -al, -ize, -ization* as variants of a single item; another says that they are four separate items. But it is possible to calculate the number of items in a college dictionary that have more than one sense. The average in the dictionaries I examined was 2.4 senses per entry. The more highly specialized a dictionary, the more monosemic it becomes. A dictionary of botany, for example, will have a figure closer to 1, but even science dictionaries contain several polysemic words. My own dictionary of linguistics,[2] for example, contains 10 per cent polysemic words. But there is another consideration: the larger the dictionary, the more polysemic it becomes, because more subtle differences of meaning come to be included that a concise dictionary would omit. In the unabridged *Oxford English Dictionary* (*OED*), approximately half the single-word headwords (excluding cross-references and hyphenated items) have more than one sense – over 200,000 headwords. And if we restrict the sample to just the commonly occurring words in the language, the figure rises to over 90 per cent. Indeed, it is difficult to find everyday words which are truly monosemic. *Dachshund* is one.

American dictionaries are even more ambiguous than British ones, because they follow a more inclusive tradition. British dictionaries (since Johnson) exclude encyclopedic words, such as names of people and places, unless they have a general meaning (such as *Whitehall*). American dictionaries (since Webster) do not. So, in *Webster's Third New International*, for example, we find an entry *Newport* consisting of three senses for *Newport* in England, *Newport* in the Isle of Wight, and *Newport* in Rhode Island. There is no entry at all in the *OED* for *Newport*. When we add words which reflect encyclopedic knowledge – names of people, places, products, organizations, and so on – to our list of words in a language, the potential for ambiguity becomes virtually 100 per cent. The word *access*, for example, has both lexical meanings (such as 'a means of entrance to a building' or 'a right to meet one's children after a divorce') and encyclopedic meanings (such as 'a credit-card firm' and 'a computer package'). In searching, the distinction between dictionary and encyclopedia disappears. Typing in 'access' to a search engine would bring up all of these senses and more. Or again: *oasis*, for a fertile spot in a desert, might have been monosemic once, but now that *Oasis* the pop group exists, not to mention OASIS, the Organization for the Advancement of Structured Information Standards, it is monosemic no longer. And a moment's search on the web brings to light the names of stores, magazines, healthfarms, and many other entities which illustrate the heavily ambiguous nature of this word today. Indeed, because virtually every word in the English language has been bought by someone as a potential domain name, it is probably true to say that the concept of an unambiguous word in everyday English will soon disappear altogether. Other online languages are being similarly affected.

Any approach to search engine disambiguation which restricts itself to a conventional dictionary is doomed to failure. A British dictionary will capture only a small proportion of the ambiguous terms which are 'out there'. An American dictionary will capture proportionately more, but will still fail miserably. A web search soon brings to light over a dozen places called *Newport*. Most of them are missing from even the largest American dictionary. But not from the largest encyclopedia – and this is the point. It is the job of encyclopedists to include all the important Newports and Oasises of the world. And that is what they do. On the other hand, encyclopedias are very bad at including explanations of the common words of a language. We will not find an entry defining most of the words in this paragraph in an encyclopedia. That is what dictionaries do.

The implication is plain. Only a combination of dictionary and encyclopedia can solve the problem of online ambiguity satisfactorily. And in a setting such as the web, where both kinds of information are inextricably mixed, only an approach to disambiguation which is grounded in both domains has a chance of being successful. Type *oasis* into Google, and no distinction is made between dictionary and encyclopedia. The various applications of the word turn up in an order totally unrelated to their meaning, but governed by ranking factors which have nothing to do with anything linguistic. Google gives us user sensitivity, but it does not give us sense. We are left to work that out for ourselves.

Purely lexical approaches, such as the various 'word-net' or 'word-map' type approaches available on the web, important as they are in making information available about word-classes, groups of synonyms, and so on, make only a small inroad into the problem of search engine disambiguation. This is because, for every one dictionary sense of a word, there are a potentially infinite number of encyclopedia senses. We can prove this to ourselves in an instant by trying to think up a new lexical sense for the word *oasis* – a figurative way of using this word, perhaps. It is difficult to do. But thinking up a new possible encyclopedic application for *oasis* – a new product name, or shop name, or whatever – is easy. People are doing this kind of thing every day of the week for a huge number of words in the language.

The conclusion is that only an encyclopedic perspective can address the problem of ambiguous searching on the web. It is a perspective which needs to integrate within itself the findings of dictionary research, so that both common words and proper names are covered. This integrated approach I refer to as *lexicopedic*.

A LEXICOPEDIC APPROACH

There are two ways of making a lexicopedia work. One is to incorporate lexical information into an encyclopedia, and this is an approach which is increasingly encountered in online reference publishing. We have all had the experience of reading an entry in an encyclopedia, but being unable to understand it because it contains too many unfamiliar words. In *The Cambridge Encyclopedia*, the entry on *fumaric acid* begins: 'An unsaturated dicarboxylic acid, used in the manufacture of polyester resins' – all well and good if we know what 'unsaturated' (etc.) means. But if we do not, we will have to turn to a dictionary to find out, for the encyclopedia may not tell us. The ideal is to have a dictionary bound in with the encyclopedia – never implementable in traditional book publishing, but now highly practicable on a computer. Click on a difficult word and the definition pops up. It is an area currently being explored by Internet lexicography.

The second approach is to incorporate encyclopedic information into a dictionary entry by giving each sense a classification. The core of this idea has long been recognized in lexicography, in the use of stylistic labels for words – we might see a label such as 'military' or 'law' after a headword, indicating that it belongs to that domain. But lexicographers have never tried to impose an encyclopedic classification on all the senses in their world – mainly because most of the words in a dictionary have no obvious encyclopedic frame of reference in which they operate. There is no real-world domain which 'owns' such words as *big, wide, do, take, go, often, regularly*, and thousands more verbs, adjectives, and adverbs. Many nouns are also 'knowledge neutral' – such as *intransigence, recognition*, and *instance*. If we try assigning encyclopedic domains to the words in *Roget's Thesaurus*, for example, the point quickly becomes apparent. Most abstract nouns are unassignable. These are the words which would not usually be the focus of a search in a search engine. Would we ever type *big* into Google? – or *do, go, choose, regularly*, or *instance*?

It would be wrong to draw the conclusion, based on these examples, that there is no point in introducing a lexicopedic approach into search. The reason is that, even if we leave out all the knowledge-neutral words and their senses, we are still left with hundreds of thousands of words and senses which *do* have a restricted use in an encyclopedic domain. They include all the proper nouns, all the abbreviations (over half a million are listed in Gale's *Acronyms, Initialisms, and Abbreviations Dictionary*), and a very large number of common noun senses – at least 130,000 – as well as many content-specific adjectives, adverbs, and verbs. These are the items which Internet users search with.

A lexicopedic approach to the word *charge* would assign its senses to the encyclopedic domains of military, electricity, crime, and finance. A similar approach to the word *depression* would recognize psychiatry, economics, meteorology, and geology. Plainly, to implement this approach, we need two kinds of knowledge: a dictionary listing all the senses of individual words in English, and a taxonomy (a hierarchical classification), derived from an approach whose breadth of coverage is commensurate with that of a general encyclopedia. The former is available for many languages in the form of unabridged dictionaries. The latter is a more difficult goal to achieve. The classification system as a whole has to include all domains of human activity, reflecting the all-encompassing character of the Internet. The point would hardly seem to be worth making, were it not for the fact that many populist approaches to knowledge classification on the web focus on consumer-oriented domains, such as cars, sex, and pop music, and omit the more difficult conceptual areas such as politics, economics, and sociology.

A hierarchical classification system is essential because, when dealing with such issues as document classification or web searching, we need to be in a position to approach the problem at the right level. Here is a fragment of one such taxonomy:

Technology
    Transport
        Roads
           Vehicles
               Cars
                  Volvos
                     Types of Volvo

If we are interested in cars in general, we do not want our search or ad to be restricted to Volvos. Conversely, if we are looking for Volvos, we do not want our search or ad results to be cluttered with hits about other makes. Similar issues are involved at all levels in the hierarchy. The lexicon which identifies each level in the hierarchy has thus got to be sufficiently distinctive to uniquely identify that level without interference from other levels.

To guarantee successful searches, therefore, an approach deriving from Internet linguistics needs to do two things. It must identify all the common words in a language that are likely search words – that is, process the lexical content of a general dictionary and a general encyclopedia – and rate all the words for their distinctiveness at the various levels recognized in an appropriately broad and deep taxonomy. 'Appropriate' here means that the categories need to relate to the nature of the problem to be solved. With an automatic document classification system, for example, the requirement may be for only a few general categories (such as those reflecting the main content areas of a newspaper archive) or for several thousand (as in a collection of pages on natural history). In an advertising context, likewise, the advertiser may be interested in targeting ads at very general topics, such as sport, cinema, and health, or at very specific topics, such as films to do with Harry Potter, Alfred Hitchcock, or Clint Eastwood (for further examples, see Chapter 9, p. 159).

The notion of *words*, it should perhaps be reiterated at this point, is an expository convenience for a diverse group of lexical elements, including word variants within lexemes (*charge, charges, charged, charging*), multi-word proper names (*New Mexico, Ford Galaxy, Richard the Lionheart*), and multi-word expressions operating as various kinds of lexical unit (*switch off, steering wheel, hand to hand, acquired taste, hammer and sickle*). Lexicological issues of this kind have usually been ignored in attempts to find a solution to problems of online search. There is a widespread but erroneous view that any sequence of letters with a space around it is a semantic unit. But ignoring the existence of multi-word lexical units can seriously affect the outcome of a search. We would not, for example, want a page with several mentions of *Ford Galaxy* to be assigned to astronomy.

THE CENTRALITY OF SEMANTICS

A fully developed applied Internet linguistics will incorporate insights from natural language processing, computational linguistics, and other areas. It must consider all the ways in which meaning is expressed or affected, through vocabulary, grammar, graphology/phonology, and discourse, and the various sociolinguistic, stylistic, and pragmatic factors affecting language use. Diachronic as well as synchronic perspectives are both essential, as we shall see below. But a semantic perspective is fundamental.

Semantic principles have to be at the heart of any linguistically based approach to online search. The focus must always be on the way one person makes sense to another. When we make sense, we demonstrate a meeting of linguistic minds. And when this does not happen, we have, literally, non-sense. Online searching at present is often non-sense, because the failures – the searches which do not give us what we want – frequently exceed the successes. Successful searching can only come from a procedure which places sense at the core of its operation. From a linguistic point of view, the notion of a search engine needs to be supplemented by that of a *sense engine*. A sense engine provides the frame of semantic reference within which a search engine can operate.

Search engines alone do not solve the problems identified above, because they do not sufficiently respect a fundamental principle of linguistic behaviour: that the primary purpose of language is to communicate meaningfully. Only in a technological world does the notion of 'a million hits' have any value. Linguistically, it is a nonsense. Nobody can make sense of a million hits, especially when they mix results from different languages. What is needed is a smaller range of highly relevant, coherent, and accurate hits – hits that make sense to an individual language user.

Searches based solely on simple statistical algorithms, such as identifying the most frequently occurring word on a page, cannot achieve the level of success that is needed. There is simply too much data on the Internet and too much complexity in the lexical system of a language to allow such algorithms to succeed, in their present state. An approach deriving from linguistics is likely to provide more promising ways of capturing the notion of sense, because linguists are familiar with the kinds of semantic complexity involved, and have developed analytical concepts and tools which bear directly on the problems.

Human intuition is central to resolving the issues. It is the adult human brain which 'knows' how words work and how they relate to each other. The native speaker of a language knows, without need of any assistance, that the word *spick* in English is invariably followed by the word *span*, or that *amok* must be preceded by the word *run*. Native speakers also know that the opposite of *fat* is *thin*, and that a *tulip* is a 'kind of' *flower*. And they know how to invent words – that *unbig* is a possible opposite of *big*, even though it is not in any dictionary. No automatic procedure has yet been devised which can capture and represent the multifarious relationships involved.

It is also native speaker intuition which 'knows' which words in a document are the ones which 'make sense' of that document, enabling the reader to distinguish its content from other documents. As the above examples indicate, the task is to be able to distinguish documents about *depression* (in the sense of weather) from *depression* (in the sense of psychiatry), *depression* (in the sense of economics), and *depression* (in the sense of a hole in the ground). Native speakers can do this instantly, because they intuitively recognize the lexical sets of which the word *depression* is an element. In documents about the weather, *depression* will be one item among several other distinctive weather-related items (see further, p. 147). In documents about states of mind, we would expect to find several other distinctive psychiatric terms.

The important thing is to capture this notion of 'distinctiveness'. Which are the most distinctive weather words, or psychiatric words? The crucial point to appreciate is that there is no simple way of doing this. There is no single statistical correlation between our awareness of semantic distinctiveness and the lexicon a document contains. For instance, it would be wrong to assume that the most frequently occurring content words in a document are always the most stylistically distinctive features of that document. It would also be wrong to assume that the rarest content words are always the most distinctive. Sometimes they are; sometimes they aren't.

The amount of polysemy presented by a word is always a factor in rating distinctiveness. Monosemic words are likely to be the most distinctive. An item such as *quarterback* makes a high-value contribution to the domain of 'American football', because it is rarely encountered outside this setting; when we see that word on a page, it is virtually certain that the page is going to be about that particular sport. By contrast, an item such as *depression* is less distinctive because it is used in four domains; and an item such as *country* has a very low distinctiveness rating, because it can be used in relation to hundreds of domains (all the countries of the world, for a start). Any sense engine has to incorporate a word's degree of distinctiveness into its operating procedure, whether this is derived from intuitive judgements or from frequency counts.

The ideal approach is therefore one which harnesses the lexical knowledge inherent in the linguistic intuition of adult users of a language and builds this into a sense engine. It does this by tapping native speakers' knowledge about the semantic relationships between words and about the contexts in which words occur. To be successful, the sense engine has to be comprehensive. Because *any* word in the language can (in principle) be part of a search enquiry, *all* words – or, at least, in the first instance, all words in general usage (i.e. excluding highly specialized terms) – have to be analysed from the point of view of their potential as discriminators of online documents.

Where do we get our words from, when we carry out a search? Two ways are typical: we can think them up ourselves; or we can choose from a set of words selected by someone else, such as the owner of a web page or a taxonomy editor. Both ways present difficulties. Self-choice runs up against the problem of lexical memory: it is not always easy to think of the words that most closely relate to what we want to find. Anyone who has had to list key words for an article knows how difficult this can be. There is always the feeling that the 'best' key words are just beyond our recall. Other-person choice runs up against the problem of matching expectation: we cannot assume that one person's selection of words identifying a topic will meet the expectations of another. Person A might think that a relevant word for a particular singer is 'jazz'; Person

B might think it is 'blues'; Person C might think it is 'folk'; and so on. No area of knowledge is immune from problems of this kind. Sources which allow taxonomies to grow spontaneously, such as the open directory DMOZ,[3] illustrate the problem, as they contain immense amounts of duplication and inconsistency.

Any solution to the problem of searching has to handle the semantics in a more scientific way. A semantic approach has to describe the polysemy of lexical items, relate the senses to a knowledge hierarchy representing online content, and assess the contribution individual lexical items make to the semantic identity of an e-text. It is not enough to say that *depression* has the four meanings noted above; we must assign each use to the knowledge domain to which it belongs. *Depression* = 'downturn in economic growth' needs to be assigned to 'economics'; *depression* = 'area of low pressure' to 'meteorology'; and so on. The factors involved are too complex to be resolvable by individual searchers or document providers, with all their memory limitations, personal preferences, and idiosyncrasies. They need to be studied objectively and systematically, and procedures need to be introduced which guarantee a comprehensive and intuitively plausible account of a language's lexicon. This is the only way in which search can ultimately 'make sense'.

AN ILLUSTRATION

We can see the process at work if we look at one of the above Internet fields in detail: the various linguistically inspired developments which have been implemented in the field of online advertising since the late 1990s. For advertisers, there is no doubt that placing their product alongside related web content is an extremely attractive proposition, for it generates a higher yield than that provided by more traditional methods. However, as the earlier examples illustrate, it has proved to be difficult to implement. The first procedures relied on single key words (such as *knife*, *gas*, *plane*), or on simple combinations of key words, to make the link between ad and page. Such a crude model cannot work, because it does not take polysemy and context into account, and the result is misassignment.

An early proposal was to put words into context. The argument went like this: the word *knife* in the stabbing report is accompanied by such other words as *police, blood, body,* and *murder.* The word *knife* in the ad inventory is accompanied by words such as *fork, spoon, cup,* and *plate.* By taking these other words into account, *knife* will be disambiguated into its 'weapons' and 'cutlery' senses. And indeed, it is possible to use this approach (often called *contextual semantics* in the online advertising industry) to distinguish senses in this way.

However, a contextual approach is only part of the solution, for it captures only part of the content of a page. The stabbing story was not really about knives, even though the word *knife* appeared there several times; the report was actually about a range of other issues, such as street safety, policing methods, and citizen protection. This is typical. Most web pages (forums, blogs, etc.) are multithematic. Our initial impression, on encountering a page, is of course the opposite: we see the headline and assume that this is what the page is 'about' – an impression that is reinforced by what we read in the first paragraph. But if we read down to the bottom of a page, other themes soon come to the fore. For example, a report on a win by a tennis star was not only about tennis, but also about cars and dating. Only by reading the whole page did this become clear. After reporting the tennis win, the writer of the article went on to talk about the star's taste in cars and women.

It is very rare to find a web page which has just a single theme. With many pages, indeed, the multithematic character is evident just by looking at the screen. In the centre we see the primary focus of the page (a report on the environment, for example), and in various places around the report window we see a selection of other topics. So if we want to see ads on the page which are relevant to its content, it is essential to have a means of analysing the content of the *entire* page. In a word, we need to know what a page is 'about', and there will be several answers. For the linguist, this is primarily an exercise in *semantic targeting* – a term which has been picked up by the online advertising world, but which is also applicable to any online enquiry in which search relevance, coherence, and accuracy are important goals.

Accuracy, however, is a shifting target. The ultimate advertising goal is to place ads on web pages so that they relate as closely as possible to the content of the page. If the page is about Britney Spears, then once upon a time it was enough simply to ensure that the ads were about music, rather than about, say, weapons (spears). Then the demand narrowed: the ads had to be about popular music, and not classical music. Then the demand narrowed further: the ads had to be about Britney Spears as such. And a further demand required yet more narrowing: some advertisers only want their Britney Spears ads to be placed on pages which say nice things about her. If a new album is given a bad review, they do not want to be associated with it. The same point applies to commercial goods. A firm X which makes washing-machines does not want to advertise on a web page or forum which says that X's washing-machines are rubbish. So now there is a new goal, which can be summed up in another single word: sentiment.

Can we identify the sentiment of a web page? It is indeed possible, but it requires another lexicographic trawl – this time identifying all the words in a language which express positive and negative attitudes. Positive attitudes would be expressed using such words as *wonderful, marvellous*, and *number 1*; negative attitudes by *awful, all-time low*, and *rubbish*. (In an analysis of sentiment expressions in a dictionary I found 1,772 positive expressions and 3,158 negative ones. It seems we have the opportunity to say twice as many nasty things as nice things, at least in English.) However, applying such an analysis to web pages is not straightforward. Many attitudinal words are ambiguous out of context (*remarkable, bewildering, incredible*). If we read that 'her performance was incredible', was it a good or a bad performance? Only when we see *incredible* in association with other words can we make a judgement. The reversative force of negative words also has to be taken into account: compare *her latest recording is bad* vs *her latest recording is by no means bad* or *his new book is his best* vs *his new book is not his best*. And there are several other syntactic considerations, involving word order and the use of intensifiers (such as *very*). An originally lexical exercise now takes on a grammatical dimension, and the research is forced to move in the direction of the kind of issue that has long been a central concern of natural language processing.

Nor is this the end of the story. Another focus of the advertising industry is behavioural profiling. Here the question is no longer 'Do people like X?' but 'Do *you*, John Doe, Mary Smith, like X?' Is it possible to tell, from an analysis of your blog, or your page on Facebook, what your interests are to the extent that a highly personalized advertising campaign can be targeted at you? I am not here concerned with the social or ethical issues involved. It is a complex arena. Speaking personally, there are some ads I would be very happy to receive, relating to my particular interests; and there are others which would irritate me enormously, and fall under the category of spam. I do not think there is much that linguistics can contribute to this issue.

The second group of examples on p. 97 (such as the plane company that advertised its services alongside a report of a crash involving one of its planes) identifies a further advertising goal: sensitivity. There are a number of Internet domains which raise problems for advertisers – for example, sites to do with smoking, drinking, gambling, weapons, pornography, and nudity; sites which report bad news; sites which present extreme views to do with politics or religion; and sites which introduce a great deal of swearing. Most advertisers (other than those which specialize in such areas, of course) do not want their ads to appear on such sites. How can misplacement be avoided? Semantic targeting, previously used in a positive way to include as much as possible, now has to be used to exclude. It is no longer a question of relevance (for planes are obviously relevant to plane crashes) but of brand protection. And it is not only the aeroplane company that wants protection. Travel agencies, hotels, tourist destinations, and other plane-related enterprises do not want to be tainted by association, by having their ads appear next to a report of a disaster.

Linguistic analysis now has to focus on the lexical character of the dangerous categories. What words are used when a page is about pornography, gambling, or bad news? Each category has to be explored to identify the lexical items which characterize it. Conventional dictionaries turn out to be of limited value in this respect: only a small amount of pornographic lexicology has so far been incorporated into the files of the *Oxford English Dictionary*, and there is a limit to the amount of contentious content that would appear in the pages of a general encyclopedia. Accordingly, the only way of obtaining a good lexical list is the direct analysis of a representative sample of web pages from each of the sensitive domains. It is not always comfortable work, it has to be said, even though linguists, like doctors, are made of stern stuff. It is quite a task handling a project involving the detailed analysis of the lexicon of these domains with equanimity, and in some cases it is virtually impossible to carry out without personal risk (see p. 123). But once an analysis has been made, the result can be used as a filter to block ads from appearing on sensitive pages. And the technology can then be used for other protective purposes, such as preventing children from accessing these pages.

OTHER ASPECTS

Although semantics has been the focus of this chapter, the implementation of any approach has to take into account several other aspects of language structure and use. I have already alluded to syntax as an important factor in disambiguation (p. 111). Word-class tagging may be needed to distinguish homographs with different senses (*bear* verb vs *bear* noun). Morphological analysis is also relevant in order to handle inflectional variants (*mobile phone(s)*) and compounding alternatives (*cellphone, cellphone, cellphone*). Some approaches use automatic morpheme stripping procedures to enable a system to work directly with lexemes.[4]

Graphology

The identity of the lexical units on a page is also dependent on an adequate graphological analysis. It is intuitively obvious that all the following examples illustrate the same word:

car   car.   car,   'car'   car's   car?

But the program has to be written in such a way that it ignores these punctuation marks, in finding the word *car* on a page, as well as other less obvious marks, such as varying numbers of continuation dots (p. 36) or varying numbers of hyphens used as a dash. There is a great deal of punctuational idiosyncrasy on the Internet. On the other hand, we do not want the program to separate car from its associated word in such strings as *carpark*, *car park*, and *'car' park*. Identifying lexemes, as opposed to words, remains one of the big challenges of automated language analysis. Other areas of graphology are also implicated, such as spelling variation (see further below), the use of accented letters and special characters, and capitalization. A word appearing in sentence-initial position will typically begin with a capital letter, which is irrelevant for the lexical identification of that word. Capital letters which identify special stylistic effects (such as *this is a Very Important Point*) also need to be disregarded. On the other hand, capitalization is an essential part of the identity of most proper names, and there are many occasions where a semantic contrast is dependent on the presence or absence of a capital, such as *this is a New York text* vs *this is a new York text*, or the thousands of homographs between names and common nouns (*Peter* vs *peter*, *May* vs *may*, *Brown* vs *brown*, etc.).

A graphological perspective is also needed to define the limits of spelling acceptability and to identify deviant spam usage (p. 71). The lexical lists needed for semantic categories have to include all permitted variations, such as dialect variation (*colour/color*, *paediatric/pediatric*) and within-region alternatives (*judgment/judgement*, *advertise/advertize*, *flower-pot/flower pot/flowerpot*, *Bible/bible*). This is no small task, as many words are involved.[5] On the other hand, we do not want to clutter up lexical lists by including typographical errors such as *comptuer* or spelling uncertainties such as *aniversary*. Occasional spelling errors on a web page are of little concern to a semantic targeting procedure which takes all content words into account, as the thematic identity of the page is derivable from the other (correctly spelled) words it contains, so accurate results can be achieved even when some of the words are unanalysable. (A similar tolerance can be extended to the analysis of speech samples through automatic speech recognition. Speech-to-text algorithms often contain errors, especially when trying to identify proper names, but they can usually provide a text of sufficient accuracy to enable an accurate semantic classification to be made.) I expect errors in written language will eventually be identified and corrected through the use of fuzzy word recognition algorithms, such as those used by some search engines to identify mistypings (*did you mean . . . ?*). A page where virtually all the words were misspelled would be a serious candidate for the spam folder.

Discourse analysis

A discourse analysis needs to be made of what is on a screen and how it is organized. If we wish to process a web page about, say, refrigerators, a typical screen shot of a retail site will display a great deal of organizational information containing lexical items that are nothing to do with refrigerators, as this brief selection illustrates:

home	help
search	top searches
about	contact
copyright	sponsored listings
sign in	my account
password	forgotten your password?
delivery	privacy policy
go to basket	terms and conditions

All this information, along with the associated programming lexicon (*sort*, *bin*, *print*, *find*, *value*, etc.) has to be discounted when the page is scraped to identify the desired text, and this is not easy. It is not a problem if the core text on refrigerators is tagged in some way, but this is often not the case. The result is that a page about refrigerators might be analysed as being 'about' computer software, simply because a large number of software terms are picked up in the scrape. If a programming solution is not available, then some sort of linguistic specification of the kinds of information present on a page is prerequisite for progress.

The complexity and variability of the metadata that supports an online page is considerable, and has been the focus of several approaches in computer science concerned to introduce standards in the way Internet resources are digitally organized. For example, the Dublin Core, developed in the mid-1990s (in Dublin, Ohio), is a widely used set of conventions for online description that facilitate search across different Internet domains, such as video, sound, images, and the various text-based outputs described earlier in this book.[6] It is called a 'core' to reflect the principle that the 15 categories in its basic metadata element set are expandable. These categories recognize page title, creator, subject, description, publisher, contributor, date, type, format, identifier, source, language, relation, coverage, and rights. Of particular linguistic relevance to the kind of problems identified above is the description, which typically includes key words supplied by the page creator saying what the page is about. These are especially important if a page has little or no textual content visible on screen.

Pragmatics

A pragmatic perspective (p. 69) is needed to take into account the way the content of a page will vary according to the intention of the page-owners or the effect they wish to convey. Why is a web page written in the way it is? What is its purpose? One page may be written purely to provide information. Another may be to persuade people to buy something. Another may be to influence opinion or (as in some racial sites) to inflame it. A page may have purely entertainment value (puzzles, games, humour, porn . . .) or exist solely to display creativity or innovation (poetry, photography, graphic arts . . .). It may exist simply as part of an ongoing conversation (as in social media). There are many possible intentions and outcomes, which will be reflected in the language and layout of the page. If the page is about buying, it will have a distinctive graphical and functional layout, including a space for making purchases (*go to basket*, etc.). Pages with extreme views will typically contain taboo language.

From a commercial point of view, a pragmatic perspective is of great potential significance, because the advertising revenues which maintain so much of the Internet are conditional on effective targeting strategies, as already noted in relation to sentiment analysis and behavioural profiling (p. 111). The effectiveness of an ad placement on a page is measured by a variety of techniques, such as *click-through rate* (CTR) – the number of times someone clicks on an ad which appears on their page, usually expressed as a percentage of the number of ad impressions delivered. If an agency delivers a thousand impressions to various web pages, and the response is ten clicks, that would be a CTR of 1 per cent. (Typical CTRs are much less than this, and any campaign which increased the CTR to more than that would be considered very successful.) A pragmatic analysis would explore the nature of the factors that raise customer expectation, generate engagement (or apathy), maintain brand presence, or elicit a good or (as in the case of insensitive ad placement, p. 112) bad public response. Incorporating information about the behaviour of Internet users, as established by available analytics programs, is an important part of this. How many pages on a site do people visit? How long do they stay on a page? How much of an online video do people watch? The more people know about online behaviour, the more they will manipulate the content of pages to best effect. If some pages (or parts of a page) are viewed more than others, advertisers will want to locate their ads there. If people do not scroll down a page, this has implications for where a web designer will place important information. Linguists need to be aware of these situational factors if they want to explain the linguistic character of what they see online.

Variation

The study of situation takes us firmly in the direction of sociolinguistics and stylistics – fields which focus on language variation. In semantic targeting, these perspectives are needed to ensure that lexical lists are truly comprehensive – for example, including formal and informal variants, regional differences (notably American vs British English, such as car *boot/trunk*), and a wide range of synonyms which express subtle variations of style. The concept of a 'car' can be expressed by *automobile, auto, car, motor, jalopy, old banger*, and dozens more. All areas of knowledge are affected.

Some Internet outputs demand a formal style of language when we speak or write; some an informal, colloquial style (e.g. *television* vs *telly* vs *TV*). Sometimes we adopt a technical style, sometimes a popular one. There are major differences between the way people use language in such domains as science, law, broadcasting, religion, advertising, and the press. Words like *plaintiff* and *heretofore* belong to the domain of law. Words like *vouchsafe* and *hallowed* belong to that of religion. Slang needs special attention, along with popular abbreviations (as encountered in texting and tweeting). Words with a scientific or technological resonance are especially common, forming over 70 per cent of the lexicon in English (p. 58).

In the case of English, global spread has added a further complication. Not only do searches have to cope with the thousands of lexical differences between British and American (*boot* vs *trunk, bonnet* vs *hood*), but there are now also Australian, South African, Indian, Singaporean, and many other 'new Englishes' which present differences of lexical usage. A search for *pavement* in the UK is equivalent to one for *sidewalk* in the US and to one for *footpath* in Australia. Regional spelling preferences also need to be taken into account (p. 114).

Any procedure which wants to improve online searching has got to be aware of variation. A search for *autos* may bring up the same results as would be found in a search for *cars* or it may not. A search for *faucets* may bring up the same results as for *taps* or it may not. A search for *advertizing* may bring up the same results as for *advertising* or it may not. We have to be alert to the existence of all these variations, and incorporate them into our approach, if our searching is to be relevant, coherent, and accurate.

A major problem with statistical models is that they ignore sociolinguistic and stylistic factors. A word which might be frequent in one variety (say, religion) might be rare in another (say, science). Without taking into account the social context in which a word appears, statements about frequency are meaningless. Native speakers, of course, have an intuition about contexts too. For example, although the word *operation* can be used in many contexts, we know that it is especially likely in the field of medicine. We also have negative knowledge – we know that the word *operator* is not likely in medicine. A surgeon carrying out an operation is not an operator. Conversely, telephone operators do not operate or carry out operations.

Stylistic issues also arise in relation to pages with figurative or rhetorical content, such as metaphor, irony, sarcasm, and other forms of expression where the language operates at different levels. If a text were significantly metaphorical, as in some kinds of poetry, then it would not classify well, in the absence of a linguistically sophisticated account of figurative expression. Fortunately, in the advertising world, figurative expression is limited in scope. It may well be that, in the middle of a football page, the writer describes rain causing the players to 'slide about like ducks on ice', but this alone would not be enough to cause the sense engine to misclassify the page as ornithology. The majority of the page would be about football, with the words used literally, and an appropriate classification would be made. Having said that, this is an area which is ripe for further research.

Diachrony

Internet linguistics is not a purely synchronic study. The linguistic content of the medium is time sensitive and always offers scope for diachronic investigation (p. 31). Each page is time stamped, even if the date at which a page was brought into being is not immediately evident. Searches give the appearance of being synchronic, though in fact they present simultaneously hits from different time-periods. Disentangling the conflicts in the data (e.g. when a series of search results gives different population estimates for a country, p. 12) is not always easy, and this problem is going to increase as the Internet archive grows.

A diachronic perspective is essential in any system of semantic targeting, because the system always needs to be kept up to date. New words are constantly being introduced into a language, and they have to be added to the lexical sets, if they are to keep pace with changes in Internet content. For example, in 1999 any set of lexical items relating to Iraq would not have included the phrase *weapons of mass destruction* – something which became necessary in 2003. Or, to take a more commercial example, as new car models come on the market, their names and model designations have to be incorporated. Keeping pace with progress in all areas of knowledge is the biggest problem facing a lexicopedic approach. For the most part, updating is carried out manually, with human editors monitoring fast-moving areas and noting new words and expressions as they arise. It is a time-consuming and error-prone solution. The field needs to work towards an automated solution, in which editors receive regular reports about changes in the index of all words online. New words would be flagged for attention, as would the disappearance of old words and changes in a word's frequency of use.

The diachronic perspective also applies retrospectively. As more historical material becomes searchable, lexical sets devised for the present-day need to be adapted to be appropriate to the earlier period. The lexical set for *road vehicles* devised for the 2000s, for example, is not going to work well when applied to a newspaper corpus relating to mid-Victorian English, with its *broughams*, *phaetons*, and *landaus*. Not only do these words have to be added; words unknown in the 1850s (such as *automobile*) have to be removed.

Diachrony also has to be taken into account in cases where pages are evolving, as in forums and social networking sites, where people are continually adding fresh material, and thus altering the semantic content of the page (p. 32). We can envisage a scenario where a page alters its semantic classification simply because the conversation moves in a fresh direction: yesterday the page was chiefly about cars; today it is chiefly about movies. Any online advertiser wishing to place relevant ads on a page would need to be made aware of the changed circumstances. A dynamic, time-sensitive approach to semantic targeting is thus required, in which pages are sampled at regular intervals and the information fed back to the client. Nor is this purely an issue for advertisers. It would affect anyone involved in automatic document classification. And it would especially affect anyone wishing to analyse the character of an evolving conversation – a situation which turns out to be of especial significance in relation to online security.

See also 'Research directions and activities', pp. 158–62.

7

A FORENSIC CASE STUDY

In several Internet situations the requirement is to identify undesirable activity on a site, such as might be carried out by fraudsters, terrorists, or paedophiles. An example of the latter is a newspaper report of a teenage girl ending up in a dangerous situation having agreed to meet offline an apparently innocent contact made during a chatroom conversation. The contact turned out to be a male predator. Several companies and agencies are now concerned to find ways of identifying potentially dangerous content within the discourse of chatrooms and social networking sites.[1] The dangers have increased following the increased provision of content via mobile phones. Parents at least had the opportunity to monitor online activity when this took place through the home computer, but this opportunity is lost when the contact is made directly to a child's mobile.

Insofar as individuals who pose a threat to public safety have to use language in order to coordinate their activities, the texts they communicate can be analysed using the same methods that are used in identifying and discriminating other knowledge domains. But there is a difference with such fields as advertising and e-commerce, where communicative intentions are transparent. When individuals plot an illegal act, they tend to use language that is coded in some way. No terrorists, fraudsters, or paedophiles are going to openly declare their intentions in plain language. The linguistic challenge is to work out which features of language provide the clues to the intentions behind the activity.

Unlike the kind of linguistic approach discussed in Chapter 6, the focus now has to be on conversation analysis. Meanings are being expressed indirectly, and the overall effect accumulates over a period of time. Individual sentences, viewed in isolation, may appear to be quite innocent. Only when viewed as part of a sequence with other sentences does a picture emerge of a hidden intention. In the case of paedophile activity, for example, the sentence *How old are you?* is innocent enough as a casual enquiry; but, seen along with such other sentences as *Are you alone?* or *What are you wearing?*, a different linguistic profile appears. We need to distinguish between innocent conversations and those which, through their use of suggestive words and sentences, build up a suspicious pattern of discourse over time.

Linguistic analyses of this kind are not easy to make, for reasons that are nothing to do with linguistics. It is difficult to obtain samples of authentic data to analyse in order to provide norms. This is a regular problem in forensic linguistics. How do paedophiles, fraudsters, and terrorists actually talk online? Applied linguists need to obtain clearance from the relevant authorities whenever they propose to engage in counter-criminal research, and that is never easy to obtain. In fact, despite several attempts a few years ago to collect a corpus in this field, I was never able to get permission to access restricted data. The illustrations in this chapter are therefore limited to a case study of paedophile conversation based on what I could find online (in 2003), made available by a child protection agency. The conversation (on an instant messaging site) was said by the agency to be typical of the genre, but no conclusions about representativeness can be drawn from such a small sample. Its value is solely to illustrate the kind of linguistic issues we have to engage with when working in the domain of online security, and to illustrate one possible solution.[2]

AN EXTRACT

This is an extract from early in a predator/victim (P/V) conversation which took place over several weeks (names have been changed from the original), at a point where P (male, age 46) is trying to engender a feeling of sympathy and rapport with a young girl (age 15). The total transcript consisted of around a thousand conversational turns.

> P: got your mail, sorry I haven't replied, rather busy at present (death of mother)
> V: oh Im so sorry
> V: I woried in case I was being too forward
> V: my gran died a couple of years ago and I remember how much that hurt
> V: It must feel pretty awful
> P: very sudden, but not in pain, still these things happen to us all at sometime or other, must not dwell on it, plenty to do and sort out
> V: yeh i bet
> V: theres not much wrong in dwelling on it though
> V: thats an Ok thing to do
> P: lets change to subject
> V: OK
> V: no prob
> P: lets change the subject
> V: k
> V: any sugestions?
> P: Tell me about you, why submissive
> V: um
> V: do you know, I dont realy know
> V: it started as a laugh and then . . .
> V: its just such a high
> V: trouble is I dont think too many people understand
> V: theres too many kids out there i gues
> P: why did it start as a laugh
> V: just from messing on the net
> P: in what way?
> V: um
> V: (thinks)

V: you want the whole thing?

P: I want to know what makes you tick

V: ok

V: thats easy

V: giveing control away is what makes me fly

V: like its my choice too, but you kinda get yourself to the point whare its a point of pride to stick with it

V: BUT

V: it needs someone whos got some life experience to take that control

V: and people like that are hard to find

P: thats true

V: you ever got involved like this before?

P: So I take it that you have had no real time experience

V: yeh I have

P: yes

V: it was another world

V: anything I do, I do for real

V: not head stuff

P: what did you experience? how did you enjoy it?

V: wow

V: this sounds like an interview!

V: lol

P: in a way yes, I need to know, if what we have in common

V: bit reluctant to get into big personal stuff with someone I dont realy know . . . . . . yet

V: but if that someone is right

V: diffrent matter

P: fair enough . . .

The turn-taking asymmetry between P and V is notable, and is characteristic of the entire conversation: two-thirds of the turns in the sample belong to V.

A CASE STUDY

There are two distinct aspects to the linguistic analysis of P data: monitoring the incoming messages from P, and advising V and others (such as V's parents) how to respond. In this respect, the distinction is similar to that found in the world of speech pathology with children, where diagnosis precedes intervention, and the therapist may then involve parents in the work. In both domains we have to establish linguistic norms and then identify linguistic features which deviate from those norms. In the present case, the diagnostic features emerged from a comparison of P/V conversations with 'innocent' conversations. Five online conversations of varying lengths were used as controls:

> an actor talking to another actor (CG1)
> a group of nine Irish adult genealogists (CG2)
> a group of nine young *Buffy the Vampire Slayer* addicts (CG4)
> two students talking about a project (CG3: S1, S2)
> three students talking about a project (CG3: N, L, S)

As with the problem areas in Chapter 6, a semantic approach seemed to be the one most likely to identify diagnostic features, in the form of the suggestive words (SW), phrases, or sentences that express P's underlying intent. Using the data in my sample, supplemented by the same kind of dictionary trawl reported earlier (p. 111), I set up a lexical scale of suggestiveness, where the words were graded in terms of a hypothesized level of predator interest, scoring from 1 to 5:

> Level 1 words: age, friend
> Level 2 words: enjoy, legs
> Level 3 words: alone, cam
> Level 4 words: bare, bedroom
> Level 5 words: breasts, meeting

Over 350 words (including variant forms, e.g. *picture*, *pictures*, *pic*, *pics*) were classified in this way. The hypothesis was that a paedophile conversation would show a steady accumulation of SWs, whereas an innocent conversation would not.

METHOD

We need a system which will identify danger early on, but not so early as to bring up incidental high-scoring usage in innocent conversations. We have to avoid misassigning cases where there is a high score at the outset because of some chance subject-matter. I therefore calculated a Cumulative Paedophile Index (CPI) for each conversational sample, taking each P utterance in turn and calculating its SW score. The score in the second utterance is added to that in the first; the score in the third utterance is added to that total; and so on. For example, in the following sequence of turns:

    if utterance 1 scores 0 the cumulative SW score is   0
    if utterance 2 scores 0 the cumulative SW score is   0
    if utterance 3 scores 2 the cumulative SW score is   2
    if utterance 4 scores 2 the cumulative SW score is   4
    and so on

The CPI was obtained by dividing the cumulative SW score by the number of utterances and multiplying by 100. Thus, in the above example:

    at utterance 1 the CPI is 0   (0/1 × 100 = 0)
    at utterance 2 the CPI is 0   (0/2 × 100 = 0)
    at utterance 3 the CPI is 66   (2/3 × 100 = 66)
    at utterance 4 the CPI is 100   (4/4 × 100 = 100)
    and so on

RESULTS AND DISCUSSION

Table 7.1 (and the associated graphs in Figures 7.1 and 7.2) shows the CPIs for the characters involved in each conversation, showing the scores at five-turn intervals. There seem to be three types of innocent conversation:

    Type 1: uses virtually no SWs
    Type 2: uses some SWs at the outset, because of the subject-matter, but they quickly decline
    Type 3: maintains a negligible level of SWs, apart from the occasional peak as the subject-matter changes

Table 7.1 shows:

Two innocent conversations of Type 1: CG2, CG4
Three innocent conversations of Type 2: S1, S2, CG1 – the
opening high scores are because people talk immediately
about meetings and pictures, which are highly sensitive
SWs
Two innocent conversations of Type 3: CG1, L
A dangerous conversation: P

Table 7.1 CPI scores, all characters

Utterances	5	10	15	20	25	30	35	40	45	50
CG1										
SW score	2	6	6	9	9	9	9	9	11	11
CPI	40	60	40	45	36	30	26	22	24	22
CG2										
SW score	0	0	0	0	0	0	0	0	0	0
CPI	0	0	0	0	0	0	0	0	0	0
S1										
SW score	11	17	19	19	19	24				
CPI	220	170	126	95	76	80				
S2										
SW score	0	9	9	9	9	9				
CPI	0	90	60	45	36	30				
N										
SW score	5	5	5	5	5	6	10	14	14	
CPI	100	50	33	25	20	20	29	35	31	
S										
SW score	0	0	0	0	0	7	7	7	9	9
CPI	0	0	0	0	0	23	20	17	20	18
L										
SW score	5	7	7	7	7	22	22	22	27	27
CPI	100	70	47	35	28	73	63	55	60	54
CG4										
SW score	0	0	0	0	0	0	0	0	3	5
CPI	0	0	0	0	0	0	0	0	6	10
P										
SW score	0	5	18	36	39	44	54	56	61	89
CPI	0	50	120	180	156	147	154	140	135	178

51–100

Utterances	55	60	65	70	75	80	85	90	95	100
CG1										
SW score	12	13	16	16	16	18	20	20	20	20
CPI	22	22	25	23	21	22	23	22	21	20
CG2										
SW score	0	0	0	1	1	4	4	9	9	9
CPI	0	0	0	1	1	5	5	10	10	10
CG4										
SW score	5	5	5	5	6	6	6	9	10	10
CPI	9	8	8	7	8	7	7	10	10	10
P										
SW score	97	97	100	109	109	109	113	118	121	121
CPI	176	162	154	156	145	136	133	131	127	121

101–150

Utterances	105	110	115	120	125	130	135	140	145	150
CG1										
SW score	20	26	26	39	39	59	59	64	64	64
CPI	19	24	23	32	31	45	43	46	44	43
CG2										
SW score	9	9	9	9	9	9	9	10	10	10
CPI	9	8	8	7	7	7	7	7	7	7
CG4										
SW score	10	10	10	10	10	15	15	15	17	17
CPI	9	9	9	8	8	11	11	11	12	11
P										
SW score	121	139	159	178	187	207	234	234	238	238
CPI	115	126	138	148	150	159	173	167	164	159

151–200

Utterances	155	160	165	170	175	180	185	190	195	200
CG2										
SW score	15	15	15	15	15	15	15	15	15	15
CPI	10	9	9	9	9	8	8	8	8	7
CG4										
SW score	23	23	25	25	25	25	25	25	30	30
CPI	15	14	15	15	14	14	13	13	15	15
P										
SW score	238	238	254	269	319	321	321	334	363	372
CPI	153	149	154	158	182	178	173	176	186	186

201–250

Utterances	205	210	215	220	225	230	235	240	245	250
CG2										
SW score	15	15	15	15	15					
CPI	7	7	7	7	7					
CG4										
SW score	32	32	32	32	32	32	37	42	42	42
CPI	16	15	15	14	14	13	16	17	17	17
P										
SW score	412	420	423	464	472	477	510	532	571	643
CPI	201	200	196	211	210	207	217	222	233	257

251–300

Utterances	255	260	265	270	275	280	285	290	295	300
P										
SW score	47	47	47	47	51	55	64	71	83	88
CPI	655	668	671	676	676	713	732	775	796	810

301–350

Utterances	305	310	315	320	325	330	335	340	345	350
P										
SW score	98	98	100	102	106	106	106	114	114	114
CPI	823	829	860	866	878	883	891	895	897	906

351–400

Utterances	355	360	365	370	375	380	385	390	395	400
P										
SW score	114	114	120	125	125	130	135	138	143	143
CPI	909	921	929	950	964	967	984	989	989	994

401–50

Utterances	405	410	415	420	425
P					
SW score	143	148	148	148	148
CPI	996	1,008	1,046	1,089	1,104

A P/V conversation has different characteristics. The contrast between P and the other characters is very clear. The sample is longer, as the recordings were made over several days, but P's score passes 100 by 15 utterances and stays there, in a peak+valley pattern. His score reaches 200 some 175 utterances later and

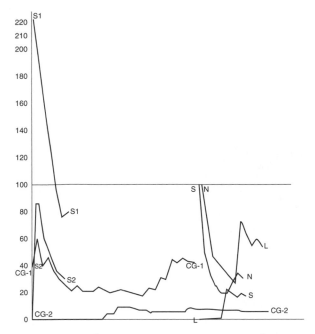

Figure 7.1 CPI scores for S₁, S₂, CG₁, CG₂, L, N, and S

rises thereafter to extremely high levels. Other characters never reach 100, which would seem to be a useful sensitivity level. An innocent conversation will routinely score well below 100. A P conversation, once it has 'taken off', will only rarely (or never?) dip below 100.

This pattern of results reflects the 'grooming' character of P interactions, in which a conversation proceeds through various stages. According to a typology proposed by Rachel O'Connell,[3] the first stage is the formation of a friendship, in which P gets to know V, and tries to develop a 'best friend' type of relationship. This is followed by a risk assessment, in which P evaluates the chances of being detected. The tempo of the conversation then changes, as P and V explore a range of topics to establish an atmosphere of secrecy and mutual trust. A variety of sexual questions of increasing intensity leads to erotic and fantasy

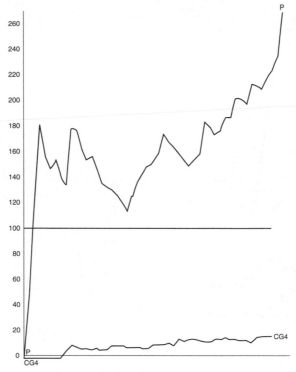

Figure 7.2 CPI scores for CG4 and P

content, in which intimacy and aggression combine, before the
online encounter is brought to an end, and an offline meeting
is arranged. In such a scenario, we would expect the number of
SWs to be low at the outset and take time to build up. P will 'test
the water' at intervals by using questions containing SWs, and
there will therefore be a pattern of peaks and valleys in the conversation. As the suggestions become more focused, some individual utterances will achieve very high SW scores, as illustrated
in Figure 7.2.

This diagnosis was based solely on the identification of individual words and expressions, without taking grammatical patterns
into account. When we move from diagnosis to intervention,

however, we need to talk in broader terms, as advice about how to respond to predator initiatives, once these have been recognized, requires an analysis in terms of sentence types, sentence sequences, and pragmatic functions.[4] In the above conversation, for example, we might identify such functions as the following, and classify P stimuli (or V responses) accordingly:

> *Setting up* V: Are you alone? Where are your parents? Where's your computer?
>
> *Identifying* V: What's your name? What school do you go to? How tall are you? What colour is your hair?
>
> *Maintaining contact with* V: Can I have your mobile number? What's your email? I'd like to text you.
>
> *Gaining V's confidence*: I'd like to know more about you. What have you been doing today? What are your hobbies?
>
> *Eliciting a description from* V: What are you wearing? Tell me what you've got on.
>
> *Eliciting action/response from* V: Can I take a photo? Will you send me a picture? Have you got a cam? What would you like me to do?
>
> *Meeting* V: Can we get together? Where would you like to meet? Have you told anyone? I don't want you to tell anyone.

What might the intervention be, in such cases? In speech pathology, the aim is to help children develop their language from where it is (delayed or deviant) to where it ought to be. In the present case, the aim is to help children develop strategies to cope with suggestive stimuli. The first step must be to alert them (or their parents or carers) to the existence of the danger. This might take the form of a series of warnings generated by the software when a conversation reached a certain danger-level. A child protection avatar might comment 'I think you should be worried about the way this conversation is going' or make a remark related to one of the grooming stages (p. 131), such as 'I don't think it's any business of his what you're wearing'. The next step could be to provide the child with alternative response strategies. It is well known that one of the difficulties in child protection is that children are unaware of the danger they are in, and may lack the experience of how to deal with suggestive questions, or believe they are in control ('I know what I'm doing'). An interesting line of linguistic enquiry would be to research a set of responses that children could choose from in order to reject suspicious advances (*That's my business*, *I don't tell people that*, *Not interested*, *Get lost!*).

Possibilities of this kind cannot be evaluated by linguists alone. Moving from diagnosis to intervention requires a collaboration, as routinely happens in several applied linguistic situations. In speech pathology, for example, clinical linguists are able to diagnose a language disability, propose hypotheses about the language goals to be introduced in therapy, and carry out an assessment of the results; but the actual task of intervention is undertaken by a cadre of professionals (speech therapists/pathologists, remedial language teachers) capable of evaluating the many non-linguistic factors that affect the welfare of the patient. The same principle applies to linguistic investigations of online security. Having diagnosed a conversation as dangerous, identified the suggestive questions, and suggested possible responses, what happens next is for others (parents, Internet service providers, child protection agencies, police) to determine. As with speech pathology, a team approach is liable to produce the best results.

See also 'Research directions and activities', pp. 161–2.

8

TOWARDS A THEORETICAL
INTERNET LINGUISTICS

The purpose of a theory is to explain something. The aim of linguistic theory is to determine the characteristics of human language, and to establish general principles for the study of all languages. It does this by developing models of language structure and use which generate hypotheses whose validity can be tested against our linguistic intuitions or with reference to observable data. The emergence of the Internet does not alter these well-established maxims of scientific investigation: it simply provides theoretical linguistics with a new domain of enquiry. The question 'Why is human language the way it is?' becomes 'Why is human language the way it is on the Internet?' And it prompts the further question: 'Does the way human language has come to be used on the Internet alter our conception of the nature of language in general?' In effect, every question linguists have asked about language, in relation to speech, writing, and sign, has to be re-asked with the qualification 'on the Internet' appended.

This book has already discussed some cases where the language we encounter on the Internet forces us to rethink explanatory principles. For example, any view of conversation which privileges the notion of simultaneous feedback has to be rethought in the light of the observation that Internet outputs typically do not permit this to happen (p. 21). The notion of the conversational turn and its associated concepts (such as the adjacency pair), which has had a central role in sociolinguistic analyses of discourse, has to be rethought to take account of the kinds of interaction observed in online chat (p. 25). The implications of imposing length constraints on the amount of written language permitted in a message (p. 33) have to be explored, for these limit the options for sentence complexity. We need to integrate new possibilities of linguistic organization into existing models – such as framing, animation, and the hypertext link (p. 28). We need to extend our conception of the possibilities of sentential expression in order to handle emoticons (p. 23). At a more specific level, we need to modify our linguistic accounts of the rules governing individual features, such as the use of the exclamation mark (p. 62), in order to cope with what we encounter online. And all of this needs to be explored in relation to a wide range of languages, to determine how universal these features are.

It is unclear how different a theory of Internet language will eventually be from the theoretical perspective which already exists for offline uses of speech, writing, and sign, because it is difficult to determine what additional constraints will be introduced by the technology. All human mediums of communication are constrained by the biological properties which manifest them – the vocal tract and ear, in the case of speech; the hand and eyes, in the case of writing; the hands, face, and eyes, in the case of sign. (I leave aside the question of which parts of the brain are involved.) In the case of writing, technology intervenes in the form of implements; but these are optional, in that it is possible in principle to write with one's fingers on a surface, such as sand or a touch-sensitive screen. With the Internet, the technology is an obligatory part of the communication situation, and its properties both extend and limit the ways in which we can operate in spoken, written, and signed language. In relation to writing, for example, it is possible to do some new things graphically on screen (such as animation), but some old things prove to be difficult or impossible, in the current state of the science (such as handwriting), and there has been considerable discussion of the extent to which there is a 'graphic untranslatability' between offline and online typography.[1] Psycholinguistic considerations also arise, as illustrated by media concern over whether our exposure to text organized in shorter visual chunks and appearing for shorter periods of time is altering our attention spans and language processing strategies – and, ultimately, the way we think (p. 55). Several other factors have been identified in earlier pages, such as the anonymity of Internet users, the multi-authorship of pages, and the uncertain boundaries of digital texts. It is not at all clear how far established linguistic theory can handle a technologically constrained medium without adaptation.

One reason for the uncertainty lies in the innocent-sounding phrase I used above: 'in the current state of the science'. A recurring theme in this book has been the rapid pace of technological innovation, and the difficulty linguists have in keeping up with the impact this has on evolving language. The obvious way for linguists to proceed is to carry out descriptions of Internet data, using already available models, and adapt the models to handle what is found. But for the reasons outlined in Chapter 1 (p. 10), the task is more difficult than we might expect. In particular, the speed of change makes linguistic descriptions out of date almost before they are finished. Already, several areas of Internet language are obsolescent, and will probably never be fully described, because the world has moved on (for example, the diverse range of MUDs and MOOs developed during the 1990s, only some of which are now operating[2]). The kind of language found on Twitter before it changed its prompt (p. 11) is likely to have been different from that currently in use – but will anyone make the effort to describe the earlier period now, rather than writing it off as a 'growing pain' of the technology? And as the viability of all new technologies is driven by revenue models, the risk for linguists, constrained as everyone else by limited time and resources, is that they might make the wrong decision about which areas to devote attention to. The press is full of stories about whether the various Internet players, especially in the social networking world, can survive – or whether, in order to survive, they need to change their business model (such as by allowing advertising). A change in business model, of course, will probably mean a change in the linguistic character of a site. Similarly, a change initiated for legal reasons (such as a concern over privacy protection, as happened to Facebook in 2010) will have linguistic consequences.

The worst case scenario is what we might call Internet language death. We can imagine the frustration of any linguist who, in 2005, decided to carry out a study of the language found on the Yahoo 360° social networking site – only to find the site closing (apart from an application in Vietnam) in 2009. In actual fact, I do not know of any linguistic study of the language of that particular output, so the example is purely hypothetical. But the underlying point is real. If nobody ever worked on Yahoo 360°, we shall never know whether some interesting linguistic features were being exploited on that site during its brief existence. Yahoo 360°, of course, is not alone. At least a dozen social networking sites have gone to the wall since the phenomenon evolved in the early 2000s. The analogy with language death is perhaps a little far-fetched; but we are certainly talking about variety death, in these cases. Even a major type of output can be affected, such as instant messaging, which was attracting predictions about its demise in 2010.[3]

We need more descriptions of outputs to provide the data from which we can construct models of Internet language, and these descriptions have to be carefully planned, to allow for the pace of change. It is not only a technologically driven change. As has been observed, social factors intervene. For example, older people become more familiar with the technology and begin to use it, introducing new styles (p. 11). Fashions change, as people develop their sense of appropriateness about the range of functions that an output can perform, as has been observed in relation to email and texting (e.g. should these outputs be used to express condolences or to sack someone?). It takes time for a new output to settle down and find its niche in the online world, as we have seen in relation to Twitter (p. 52). And an important variable is the way manufacturers alter the linguistic character of an output as they improve their products. A small but illustrative example is in the language heard on car satellite navigation (GPS) systems. In the early version of one such system, the voice of the navigator gave such instructions as:

Drive three miles, then turn left.
Drive two miles, then turn left.
Drive one miles, then turn left.

(The disregard for the concord rule with *one* had its written analogy on screens which tell us that *1 files* has been downloaded.) In a different version, the concord was respected (*Drive one mile, then turn left*), at a stroke lowering the blood pressure of innumerable car-driving pedants.

Another complication for linguistic descriptions is that the Internet is bringing linguists into contact with areas of communication that they would normally disregard as being non-linguistic in character. Internet linguistics looks as if it will develop into an Internet semiotics, becoming increasingly diverse in the range of communicative options it subjects to analysis. Under the heading of *multimodality*, we find the various ways in which users interact with the technology, such as keyboard, mouse, touch, gesture, speech, pen, and head or eye movement. Under the heading of *multimedia* we find the use of text, speech, music, animation, art, video, still photography, and various forms of interactivity (as in a video game), with progress being made in relation to taste, smell, and touch (haptic) technologies. From a linguistic point of view these developments place language in a fresh set of contexts. In a multimedia world, it is not possible to focus exclusively on the spoken or written element, treating everything else as marginal – as non-linguistic extras. All the elements combine in a single communicative act, and their joint roles need to be considered. The point can be illustrated by this instant messaging exchange between two people (P, Q) in which P introduces a hyperlink to a piece of video (LINK1) and Q responds with another (LINK2):

P   take a look at LINK1 and tell me what you think
     the costumes look familiar
     and brave new world? i think not
Q   give me a LINK2 any day

What is notable is the way both parties incorporate the links into the syntax of their sentences. P also refers to the content of the link anaphorically: there is nothing else in the discourse which can explain *the costumes*, and the phrase *brave new world* is a quotation from LINK1. P's practice has some similarities with a traditional piece of writing in which the author alludes to the content of an accompanying picture, but here any of the other media (animation, audio, etc.) can be the focus of the link, and I can think of no precedent in offline writing for the way these links have been incorporated into the dialogue.

The absence of good up-to-date descriptions is the main reason for the growth in popular mythology about Internet language, such as the view that it is causing increased illiteracy. As noted earlier (p. 4), in the absence of facts, impressions rule; and language idiosyncrasies are exaggerated and given a stature that is not warranted by their frequency of use. Only clear experimental findings, such as the influence of text-messaging on literacy,[4] and comprehensive linguistic descriptions can eventually eliminate the myths. And the exercise needs to be repeated for all speech communities where the Internet has become a routine part of daily life, for the 'moral panic' about language on the Internet is by no means restricted to English speakers.

The importance of developing a comparative linguistic dimension for Internet research cannot be stated strongly enough. The examples in this book are taken predominantly from English, and they need to be supplemented by studies from as wide a range of languages as possible. How do Internet technologies impact on languages whose grammar and orthography are very different from English? Are the linguistic strategies used by English-speaking netizens also found in other languages?[5] It is essential to broaden the language base, in order to develop a valid Internet linguistics. This is how linguistics developed as a subject in the early twentieth century, and it is the way the subject must continue to develop in the twenty-first.

RELEVANCE AND INDEXING

Any explanation of why Internet language is the way it is must make *relevance* a key principle. The notion has been given a thorough explication in the context of pragmatics by Dan Sperber,

Deirdre Wilson, and others.[6] For them, an input (such as an utterance, a search engine result) is relevant to an individual 'when it connects with background information he has available to yield conclusions that matter to him . . . when its processing in a context of available assumptions yields a positive cognitive effect . . . a worthwhile difference to the individual's representation of the world'. Based on this definition, they identify two principles: their *cognitive principle* states that 'human cognition is geared to the maximisation of relevance'; their *communicative principle* states that 'utterances create expectations of optimal relevance'. These principles are clearly operating in the various applied linguistic domains discussed in Chapter 6, and they are needed to explain or evaluate crucial kinds of Internet activity, such as the creation of semantic threads in online forums, the notion of contributions being 'off-topic', the maintenance of coherence in instant messaging exchanges, the evaluation of messages as constituting spam, and – most critically – the process of web indexing which underlies all kinds of search.

The fact that search engines produce diverse results has already been noted in Chapter 5, in the context of assessing the multilingual character of the web. But the issue is a more general one. Automatic indexers (often referred to as crawlers or spiders) process only a fraction of available web pages – between 2 per cent and 16 per cent, in one early study[7] – and use very different procedures to index the pages they find. This can be easily demonstrated by making the same search using a range of search engines. For example, Table 8.1 shows the number of hits (in millions) obtained using the search terms *linguistics* and *phonetics* in these four services.

Table 8.1 Number of hits for the search terms *linguistics* and *phonetics* on four search engines

	linguistics	*phonetics*
http://uk.yahoo.com	62.2 m	8.1 m
http://www.google.com	16.4 m	1.8 m
http://www.bing.com	12.1 m	0.9 m
http://www.ask.com	3.2 m	0.4 m

Now compare the top ten hits for the *linguistics* search shown in Table 8.2. Wikipedia aside, there is little parallelism. Edinburgh and University College London appear three times each, and Answers, Cambridge, and Intute twice, but at very different rankings.

Applying the notion of relevance to such lists is difficult, because the notion of ranking implies a quantification of the degree of relevance, and this requires knowledge of why the search was made in the first place. We will reach different conclusions depending on whether we want information about the subject in general or about departments of linguistics, for example.

Internet indexing is unlike any other kind of indexing. To see this, consider the task facing human indexers as they deal with a book. Indexers are trying to second-guess what readers will want

Table 8.2 Top ten result rankings for *linguistics* on four search engines

	Yahoo	Google	Bing	Ask
1	Wikipedia	Wikipedia	Wikipedia	Wikipedia
2	Answers	Wikipedia	Wikipedia	Edinburgh
3	Wikipedia	Intute	Edinburgh	University College London
4	School of Oriental and African Studies	Cambridge	Freebase	Linguistic Abstracts
5	Answers	Puzzles	University College London	British Association of Applied Linguistics
6	Oxford	Edinburgh	Intute	Linguistics Association of Great Britain
7	Cambridge	University College London	Glossary	French Dictionary
8	Essex	Institute of Linguists	Bangor	Routledge
9	Citizendium	BUBL	Queen Mary Information Service	Lancaster College
10	Leeds	Quality Assurance Agency	Sussex	Manchester

to find. They do not want their entries to be too general or too detailed. And they want readers to feel that their entries are relevant to their concerns. Relevance is critical. What would happen if we dispensed with it? Here is the index to a text in which no attention is paid to relevance at all. It is the opening paragraph from the Preface of my book *By Hook or By Crook*:

> The inspiration for *By Hook or By Crook* came from reading W G Sebald's *The Rings of Saturn*, an atmospheric semi-fictional account of a walking tour throughout East Anglia, in which personal reflections, historical allusions, and traveller observations randomly combine into a mesmerising novel about change, memory, oblivion, and survival. The metaphor of the title – Saturn's rings created from fragments of shattered moons – captures the fragmentary and stream-of-consciousness flow of the narrative.[8]

If we have dispensed with relevance, then we must index everything – for everything is potentially relevant. That would produce a result something like this (I am not concerned with the way these entries are phrased, only with the selection). There are 37 items in a comprehensive index of this paragraph.

account, of *The Rings of Saturn*
allusions, historical
atmosphere, of *The Rings of Saturn*
By Hook or By Crook
capture, of narrative flow
change, nature of
creation, of planetary rings
East Anglia
flow, in narrative
fragmentation, in narrative
fragments, of moons
history
inspiration
memory, nature of
mesmerising, nature of novel
metaphor
moons, shattered

narrative
novel, mesmerising
oblivion, nature of
observations, traveller
personal, nature of reflections
randomness
reading
reflections, personal
rings, of Saturn
Rings of Saturn, The
Saturn
Sebald, W G
semi-fiction
shattering, of moons
stream-of-consciousness
survival, nature of
titles, book
tour, walking
travelling
walking

To restore some sense, and reduce the number of entries, we have to reintroduce the notion of relevance. And to do that, we have to have made a judgement of what the book is about. If we know the book is about, say, astronomy, then we might index *rings* and *moons*, because we would expect there to be sub-entries in due course:

moons,

> shattered
> unshattered etc.

If we know the book is about creative writing, we might index *stream-of-consciousness* and *narrative* (among others), for the same reason:

stream-of-consciousness,

> in astronomy
> in novels etc.

We know that *rings* and *moons* are incidental (of negligible relevance) to a book on creative writing. And vice versa: we know that the notion of *narrative* is incidental to a book on astronomy.

If we cannot make a judgement of what the book is about, then we cannot easily index it. That is why fiction is so difficult to index: its content cannot be so easily reduced to a single theme, and this makes us pause as we consider what items to select for indexing. And that is why a general reference book, such as the *Penguin Factfinder*, was so hard to index.[9] Because it dealt with everything, I wanted to index everything, and that was not possible. Considerations of length, cost, and time forbade it – as it was, the index came out at 140 pages (about 15 per cent of the book).

And that is why it is so difficult to index the Internet in a sensible way. The Internet is about everything. And many individual sites and pages are about everything – in the sense that their content is totally unpredictable. Most blogs are like this. They talk about whatever topic happens to come up, day by day. Social networking sites such as Facebook are like this, as are broadcasting sites such as YouTube. But it is not just these personal sites which are multithematic. Most news sites are too, as this selection of headlines from CNN illustrates. First, two-theme:

> *Ex-Tiger Fielder says he plans to repay debts* (baseball, finance)
> *Schwarzenegger backs stem cell plan* (politics, medicine)
> *Exotic frog invades Georgia* (animals, USA)
> *Tumor may be linked to cell phone use* (phones, medicine)
> *Infection risk grows for Hong Kong* (medicine, China)

Now three-theme:

> *Company blasts ashes into space* (space, economics, death)
> *Chinese showcase fuel-saving care* (cars, China, energy)
> *AirAsia, Malaysian Air discuss cooperation* (air travel, Malaysia, politics)

And sometimes even four-theme:

Student killed during postgame celebration: woman hit by projectile fired by officer; police take full responsibility (baseball, policing, education, safety)

These are examples where the themes are explicit at the outset. Rather more subtle are those where themes are 'buried' in the body of the text. A news item might begin by reporting on a film star's latest movie, but half-way down begin to talk about his impending divorce or his eating habits or whatever. When we take all these possibilities into account, it turns out that it is relatively unusual to find a web page which is strictly monothematic (p. 110).

There are basically two approaches to indexing 'out there', and neither captures the multithematic character of the web. One is *index maximalism* – the search engine approach. The software indexes everything apart from a few stop words, such as *the*. The strengths and the weaknesses of this are evident. If our query is highly specific, we will get a useful result. Finding Ford Galaxys or Tom Cruise is easy. But if it is not, we will get millions of diverse results, and huge amounts of irrelevance. Finding information on, say, 'main universities in France which teach linguistics' proves to be, if not impossible, then so difficult that it exceeds the bounds of patience. The more abstract, wide-ranging, ambiguous, or metaphorical our enquiry, the more we will end up frustrated. It is not that the pages aren't there. It is just that they have not been indexed in a way which anticipates the relevance needs of the user.

The other approach is *index minimalism* – an approach found in online advertising, where teams of people scrutinize web pages and make a judgement about what they are about, so that a relevant ad can be placed on the screen. It is an approach which is prone to disaster, as has already been illustrated by the examples of ad misplacement in Chapter 6, such as the CNN news report about the street stabbing where the ads down the side said 'Buy your knives here . . . Get your knives on eBay' (p. 97).

Notice that the maximalist approach cannot solve the minimalist one. If the CNN report has a thousand words, then each of these words could be a trigger for an ad. If it happened to mention that the victim's *sweater* was covered in blood, then that might generate ads for knitwear. Someone has to go through the report and decide what the report is about and identify which words best capture that aboutness. It has to be a someone. No machine can yet do this. And even humans find it difficult, because there are lots of distracting words in a news report – even on a page which you might think of as monothematic, such as a science page.

To illustrate, consider this paragraph, taken from a website on weather:

> Depressions, sometimes called mid-latitude cyclones, are areas of low pressure located between 30° and 60° latitude. Depressions develop when warm air from the sub-tropics meets cold air from the polar regions. There is a favourite meeting place in the mid-Atlantic for cold polar air and warm sub-tropical air. Depressions usually have well defined warm and cold fronts, as the warm air is forced to rise above the cold air. Fronts and depressions have a birth, lifetime and death; and according to the stage at which they are encountered, so does the weather intensity vary.[10]

Which words identify the topic of 'depression'? Some, such as *cyclone*, *warm front*, and *cold front*, are clearly highly relevant – they are hardly ever used outside of this context. Others, such as *birth*, *lifetime*, and *death*, are clearly irrelevant – part of the literary style, but not the topic. And others are of uncertain relevance: *intensity*, *vary*, *areas*, *meeting place*, *mid-Atlantic*, *cold air*, all of which can be used in several other contexts in the language – *cold air* in relation to air-conditioning, for example, or *mid-Atlantic* in relation to yacht racing. Nor are the terms *front* and *depression* by themselves as helpful as you might think, for they have many other meanings in English. Indeed, type *depression* into Google and you will be swamped with advice about how to cure your mind (p. 107).

Nonetheless, it ought to be possible to rank the words on a page roughly in order of relevance, with (in this example) *cyclone* towards the top and *the* towards the bottom, and this is what needs to be done if we are to solve the problem of indexing multithematic pages or sites. Professional indexers are best placed to do this, of course, as indexing is, more than anything else, a matter of judging relevance. But indexing is really a domain of applied linguistics.

NEW DIRECTIONS

Currently, there are probably as many foetal theories of Internet language behaviour around as there are linguists. There is no such thing as a single theoretical approach, as the selection of further reading (p. 171) illustrates. However, the preoccupation with issues of description and methodology has not prevented the development of an applied Internet linguistics, as we have seen (Chapters 6 and 7). And ironically, the need to provide solutions in applied fields has brought into relief several notions (such as relevance and appropriateness) which will have a central role to play in any theory about why Internet language is the way it is. This is not the first time that an applied linguistic perspective has motivated fresh thinking in areas of theoretical linguistics, of course. To take just one field: work with patients with language disorders has informed research into neurolinguistics and psycholinguistics. But it is unusual to find so many applied fields evolving in the absence of anything resembling a coherent theory. The explanation is obvious: whoever pays the piper calls the tune and sets the deadlines. In the highly competitive world of the Internet, the products always need to be there yesterday.

Nor has the lack of an Internet linguistic theory prevented the development of an educational approach to Internet language in schools, colleges, and businesses, and among the public at large. The motivation can be summed up in the word *management*. People have to learn to manage the technology and the resources of the Internet, and part of this is an awareness of the properties of the language found there. A widespread lack of awareness is evident from the stories which regularly achieve a media presence, when people use the Internet to say things they wish they hadn't, copy messages inadvertently, or regret the posting of a personal photograph. The proliferation of netiquette guides has been an attempt to meet the need for advice about how to proceed.[11]

In schools, teachers have begun to familiarize students with the linguistic issues involved. One of the most noticeable features of Internet language is its greater informality. Languages always allow a contrast between formal and informal modes of expression, but the Internet seems to have extended the informal end of the stylistic spectrum. Certain outputs now display a level of informal usage, in the form of nonstandard spelling, capitalization, and punctuation, which would not have been encountered in the informal writing of a generation ago. The fashionable status of this level of writing makes it appeal to young people, who run the risk of generalizing the behaviour to writing contexts where it would be inappropriate. Accordingly, some teachers now do routine Internet work in their classes, where the aim is to make students aware of the situations where Internet informality would be appropriate and those where it would not. Stylistic 'translation', for example, is an illuminating technique (p. 6): students are asked to rewrite a text-message in the style of a newspaper report – or vice versa – and to reflect on the reasons for the differences. Of course, to run a class like this, teachers must themselves be aware of the properties of electronically mediated communication, and of the range of varieties which exist within it – and this awareness is by no means universal. It will take time before the findings of an Internet linguistics become a routine part of student and teacher training. In the meantime, it can be illuminating to explore some of the research directions involved in the subject, and these are illustrated in Chapter 9.

The Internet is the largest area of language development we have seen in our lifetimes. Only two things are certain: it is not going to go away, and it is going to get larger. The challenges facing linguists are considerable, as they move towards the goal of formulating a sophisticated theoretical and applied Internet linguistics. But that, of course, is the basis of its appeal.

9

RESEARCH DIRECTIONS AND ACTIVITIES

The Internet offers linguists a huge number of research opportunities. It is such a novel, diverse, and large phenomenon that students at any level are virtually guaranteed to make interesting discoveries when they explore a topic. The downside, of course, is that there may be little or no previous literature on the topic for them to use as a model. I am often approached by students wanting to explore a particular topic in Internet linguistics who ask if anything has been published on it already. In most cases, I know of nothing, and can only suggest they explore the indexes of online journals – such as the *Journal of Computer-Mediated Communication* or *Language@Internet* – to see what is there.[1] The more languages they are able to read, the more they will find, as a great deal of relevant material is published in languages other than English. I am always conscious of my own other-language limitations, when it comes to compiling an Internet linguistic bibliography.

In this chapter, I bring together a number of suggestions for activities which will increase awareness of what is involved in doing Internet linguistics. Some activities focus on replicating or extending the topics mentioned in earlier chapters; some introduce areas not already covered. In all cases, it does not take long before one develops a sense of exploring uncharted territory.

1 DEBATING ROLES (CHAPTER 1)

Arguments about standards of language usage usually reflect the non-linguistic ideologies of the participants. Use the Internet to find examples of the debate surrounding the role of the various Internet outputs in society, and discuss the extent to which the various comments reflect an ideology that goes well beyond language. As an illustration of the kind of comments people make, here is a selection from those who sent messages to an online forum about the possible demise of instant messaging (p. 4):

> People want to show off to all their hundreds of friends rather than have conversations with just one or a few people at a time.

> As someone who happens to be deaf, I find IM a real boon to communication with my parents

> What about the intrusive nature of IM? As soon as you log on you can be inundated with various conversations which ruins any other kind of web activity you are trying to get on with.

> Texting has taken the place of IM. These users are not necessarily in front of a computer all day, but cellphones are always on the table or in the pocket ready to respond to the vibration of a new text-message.

> I find social networks a pointless soul-sapping waste of time and still use IM to keep in touch with friends and family as it's simple and (as the name suggests), instant.

> Corporate decisions to block IM in the workplace have effectively killed this method of communication. A shame, seeing as more progressive employers harness it to encourage global teamworking with incredible effect.

2 AUDIO ISSUES (CHAPTER 2)

Record an audio conversation using one of the VoIP (voice-over-Internet) systems, and determine the extent to which latency factors interfere with conversational rhythm (p. 17). When speech is transmitted over the Internet, it is broken down into small packets, each containing an address telling the network routers where to send it to. When these packets reach the receiver's computer, the data is reassembled into its original state. But because the various packages have been sent along a variety of different paths, problems of transmission or reassembly can occur, so that all or part of a message is delayed, or a sequence of messages is received out of order. The delay does not have to be very great before it disrupts speaker–hearer collaboration.

Evaluate the efficiency with which automatic speech recognition devices operate. For example, SpinVox is a system which takes a voice message left on an answering machine and converts it into text, sending the result to a visual display device, such as an inbox, wall, or blog.[2] Another example: Bury Technologies produces hands-free car kits with such functions as voice dialling and text-to-speech facilities (for reading aloud incoming text-messages), and claims that they can be used without preliminary individual voice training.[3] The main problems all such approaches face are linguistic: how to handle regional accent and voice quality variations; how to exclude extraneous noise; how to cope with variations in the rate of speech; and how to deal with proper names. It is an interesting exercise for phonetically skilled linguists to systematically introduce variations in their input to such devices (such as altering their speech rate) to test the manufacturers' claims.

3 DISTINCTIVE FORMS (CHAPTER 2)

One of the major myths about Internet language is that it is preponderantly deviant. Choose an output from any language, collect a small corpus of data, and identify the words that critics of the medium cite in this connection, such as abbreviations (*lol*), words with omitted letters (*xlnt*), logograms (*2day*), nonstandard forms (*wot*), and typing errors. Count all the words in the sample and then all the nonstandard forms. How does the result compare with the proportions reported in the literature, such as those I report for text-messaging,[4] which were between 6 and 20 per cent?

In a group study, take similarly sized samples from different outputs, such as a chatroom, a blog, an instant messaging exchange, texting, Facebook, and Twitter, and compare the results for each. If the information is available, differentiate male/female or age-related usage. For example, in a school environment, there are likely to be noticeable differences in the use of textisms as one moves up through the age levels, with older students using fewer distinctive forms and writing texts that are increasingly standard in form.

Compare the set of emoticons available for use in one of the outputs, and explore pages from that output to establish just how many of these symbols are actually used, and how often. How easy is it to determine why an emoticon is used? Can social factors explain some of the differences?

Neologisms are one of the distinctive features of some Internet outputs (p. 58). Choose an output and make an alphabetical list of the terms you consider to be neologistic. Or go to one of the online dictionaries and use the lists they provide, such as Twictionary or Twittonary.[5] What types of word formation do you see in the list? What proportion of the neologisms are purely ludic in character? How many do you think are likely to have a long-term future in the language?

4 TESTING HYPOTHESES (CHAPTERS 2 AND 3)

Find a log of an instant messaging or chatroom exchange and describe the pattern of turn-taking, along the lines of p. 25. Is the degree of misunderstanding similarly low? What interaction techniques do participants use to maintain their sense of discourse organization? Are the strategies predominantly semantic or grammatical? Map the semantic threads introduced into the discourse, and explore their relationship to grammatical features such as ellipsis and anaphora. To what extent do these exchanges reflect what happens in face-to-face conversation? For example, is there any evidence of the use of comment clauses (e.g. *you know*, *you see*, *mind you*) in Internet exchanges (p. 22)?

Choose some of the parameters in the description of Twitter in Chapter 3, and test the findings against a small corpus of your own, using *language* as the search term. Carry out a similar analysis, but use a search term that has different stylistic properties, such as *dude* or *wanna* ('want to'). Does this alter your pattern of results? (Note that, as Twitter is continuously updating, your selection will be lost to view as soon as you refresh the page. Print out your corpus as soon as you have chosen it, so that you have a record of it.)

5 PUNCTUATION (CHAPTER 4)

Write a set of rules which would account for all the punctuation marks on a web page (p. 61). Be prepared to go well beyond the traditional set (commas, colons, etc.) to include section marks, dividers, slashes, and other conventions. Are some traditional marks unused? Look out for cases where a mark is missing where you might expect it to be present (e.g. in captions), or where there is inconsistency (e.g. in the amount of space surrounding a dash). Don't ignore tables, diagrams, logos, and other pictorial material. Are URLs a special case?

Carry out a graphic translatability exercise with a conventionally printed text, such as a newspaper or magazine. Are there marks which are not used online (different lengths of dash, for example)? Conversely, are there online marks which are not used in print or used in a different way – such as the use of hash (#), @, and carets (^). The Wikipedia entry at *punctuation* has a good listing, but note the fuller Unicode lists.[6] To what extent are the functions of punctuation supplanted through other graphic devices, such as white space, colour, or animation?

Adopt a sociolinguistic perspective. Are there differences between outputs in the choice and range of punctuation marks. In social networking forums, are there differences in use between male and female users? Following the example of blogging on p. 69, find some blog posts and determine the extent to which they respect traditional punctuation conventions.

6 SPAM (CHAPTER 4)

Here are 30 examples of the subject lines of spam messages (p. 71). If you had to write a spam filter to exclude such messages from your computer, what grammatical, lexical, or orthographic factors would you pay special attention to?

LASER PRINTER TONER
The Hottest Site on the Net!!
ONE-POUND-A-DAY DIET
$1,000 for sending an email
What is in it for you?
Put your subject line here
CONTROL YOUR WEIGHT
Get Rich Click
An Important Decision You Must Make
Please Read! This is not Spam!
Free Shopping Cart For Your Website
UNIVERSITY DIPLOMAS
Getting better all the time!
Just read this!
Dear Valued Customer
BOOST Your Website's Traffic
Free Service
IT TRAINING
Special Discount Offers
Christmas Gift
Free UK Delivery
SALE 75% off on drugs
She need it!
Good news!!!
Buy now Viagra
VIRUSES ALERT
Hello Mr David
Dont miss giweaways
Confirm please
Warning

7 ONLINE TRANSLATION (CHAPTER 5)

Many Internet pages now offer an automatic written text translation facility, and in February 2010 Google announced its plans for a speech facility that would allow real-time translation between people with android smartphones – a development that has been likened to the Babel fish of Douglas Adams' *Hitchhiker's Guide to the Galaxy*. Success will depend on a seamless combination of three technologies: automatic voice and speech recognition, text translation, and text-to-speech synthesis.[7]

Automatic translation has some way to go before it can achieve the level of semantic accuracy and stylistic appropriateness achieved by professional translators and interpreters. Automatic translations are quite good at conveying the gist of a document, but do not operate well when sentence structure gets at all complex or elliptical, or the text uses idiomatic or figurative expressions. Even quite basic grammatical properties can be misrepresented, and pragmatic factors not taken into account (such as an appropriate choice of pronoun in languages that have a T/V system).

Use the following extracts (the introductory paragraph from the UNESCO website in May 2010) to evaluate the efficiency of an online translation system, or carry out a similar exercise using texts and a system of your own choice. It is important to test texts operating with different stylistic properties, such as scientific and imaginative writing, for translating systems perform less efficiently the more the language uses dialogue or becomes colloquial or poetic.

Original text in English

UNESCO works to create the conditions for dialogue among civilizations, cultures and peoples, based upon respect for commonly shared values. It is through this dialogue that the world can achieve global visions of sustainable development encompassing observance of human rights, mutual respect and the alleviation of poverty, all of which are at the heart of UNESCO'S mission and activities.

Original text in French

L'UNESCO s'emploie à créer les conditions d'un dialogue entre les civilisations, les cultures et les peuples, fondé sur le respect de valeurs partagées par tous. C'est par ce dialogue que le monde peut parvenir à des conceptions globales du développement durable intégrant le respect des droits de l'homme, le respect mutuel et la réduction de la pauvreté, tous ces points étant au coeur de la mission de l'UNESCO et de son action.

Original text in Spanish

La UNESCO obra por crear condiciones propicias para un diálogo entre las civilizaciones, las culturas y los pueblos fundado en el respeto de los valores comunes. Es por medio de este diálogo como el mundo podrá forjar concepciones de un desarrollo sostenible que suponga la observancia de los derechos humanos, el respeto mutuo y la reducción de la pobreza, objetivos que se encuentran en el centro mismo de la misión y las actividades de la UNESCO.

Original text in Russian

ЮНЕСКО работает над созданием условий для диалога между цивилизациями, культурами и народами, основывающегося на уважении общих ценностей. Именно посредством этого диалога мир может придти к глобальному пониманию устойчивого развития, охватывающего соблюдение прав человека, взаимное уважение и уменьшение бремени нищеты – все это составляет суть миссии и деятельности ЮНЕСКО.

Automatic translation from French to English

The UNESCO employs itself to create the conditions of a dialog between the civilizations, the cultures and the peoples, based on the value respect divided by all. It is by this dialog that the world can succeed in global conceptions of the sustainable development integrating the respect of the human rights, the mutual respect and the reduction of poverty, all these points being at the heart of the mission of the UNESCO and of his action.

Automatic translation from Spanish to English

The UNESCO work by creating favorable conditions for a dialogue among the civilizations, the cultures and the towns based on the respect of the common values. It is through this dialogue as the world will be able to forge conceptions of a sustainable development that suppose the observance of the human rights, the mutual respect and the reduction of the poverty, objective that are found in the same center of the mission and the activities of the UNESCO.

Automatic translation from Russian to English

The UNESCO works above creation of conditions for dialogue between civilizations, cultures and people, based on respect of the general values. By means of this dialogue the world can come to global understanding of the steady development covering observance of human rights, the mutual respect and reduction of burden of poverty – all this makes an essence of mission and activity of UNESCO.

8 LOCALIZATION (CHAPTER 6)

The examples of inappropriate ad placement in Chapter 6 are all from English, but ads of course can be found in any language, and raise similar issues. Evaluate the appropriateness of the ads on a sample of web pages in a language you know. Remember to take into account the distinction between site and page: an ad may work well on a home page, but not so well on one of the constituent pages (or vice versa).

In principle, each language can develop its own taxonomy and associated linguistic analysis to handle such cases. In practice, for a mixture of business, technical, and legal reasons, the approach a company has found to work for one language is likely to be extended to others. There will have been considerable investment costs, for lexicological research is expensive in terms of both time and personnel, and the company will wish to make savings. It will also want to reuse its software package as far as possible. And a new project may require fresh legal exploration costs, to check for such issues as patent infringement.

At first sight, applying a taxonomy devised for one language to others seems to be a straightforward exercise in translation, in which lexical equivalences are found for the terms in the hierarchy and the items in the lexical lists. However, the matter is complicated by the need for cultural *localization* (p. 82). It is a commonplace of translation studies that words in one language do not always semantically match the words in another, the proportion being affected by both cultural and linguistic distance. In the case of the lexical lists described in Chapter 6, about three-quarters of the items were capable of one-for-one translation from English into other European languages. The meteorological sense of *depression* neatly equated to a corresponding word in French, German, and so on; but in around a quarter of cases there was no direct one-to-one translation, for a mixture of linguistic and cultural reasons. Semantic mismatch is a familiar issue in translation theory, summed up by the popular saying 'The French (or whoever) have a word for it'. Cultural mismatch can be illustrated by the task of translating the names of popular cigarette brands or drinks, which vary from country to country, or by the task of finding what the cultural equivalents are for political or minority groups, especially when the names are used in insulting ways.

Find a web page in English that illustrates one of the sensitive categories illustrated in Chapter 6 (such as smoking, alcohol, or extreme views), list the salient words and expressions, making sure to include encyclopedic as well as linguistic items (e.g. brand names of drinks or cigarettes), and establish an equivalent list in a language you know. Note the types of mismatch, and how many changes you have to make. Does the amount of cultural difference between the languages in your sample resemble the proportion encountered in my project? In a group study, choose pages from different web categories and establish the extent to which localization is affected by subject-matter.

9 TAXONOMY (CHAPTER 6)

Taxonomies always reflect an ideology. Here are examples of the top level of classification of four taxonomies. Knowing only what you see in these lists, what might be deduced about the aims and interests of the taxonomy creators?

A is the Dewey system widely used in libraries.[8]
B is the DMOZ open directory system referred to on p. 109.[9]

C is the system used in the *Cambridge Encyclopedia*, which was adapted for use in the project described in Chapter 6. D is Google's product taxonomy.[10]

A
Generalities
Philosophy and psychology
Religion
Social sciences
Language
Natural sciences and mathematics
Technology
The arts
Literature and rhetoric
Geography and history

B
Arts
Games
Kids and teens
Reference
Shopping
World
Business
Health
News
Regional
Society
Computers
Home
Recreation
Science
Sports

C
The universe
The earth
The environment
Natural history

Humanity
Recreation
Society
The mind
Human history
Human geography

D
Animals
Arts and entertainment
Baby and toddler
Business and industrial
Cameras and optics
Clothing and accessories
Electronics
Food, beverages and tobacco
Furniture
Hardware
Health and beauty
Home and garden
Luggage
Mature
Media
Office supplies
Software
Sporting goods
Toys and games
Vehicles and parts

10 SEMANTIC TARGETING (CHAPTERS 6 AND 7)

Develop a sense of the difficulty involved in developing a semantic targeting system for use in such areas as online search. Choose a category with which you are familiar (e.g. refrigerators, tennis, Paris, Clint Eastwood), find some web pages about it, and compile a list of the words and expressions that could be part of a semantic filter which would accurately identify that page. For example, your list for tennis might begin with *doubles*, *tennis racket*, *net*, *forehand*, *Wimbledon*, *Grand Slam*, and *Roger*

Federer. What proportion of the items in your list are unique to the category? Use a dictionary or encyclopedia to determine differences in the level of ambiguity in the polysemic items: is *net*, for example, more polysemic than *doubles*?

In a group situation, each member should compile a list for a particular category. The other members of the group are then asked to write a short article (of a hundred words or so) about the topic. How many items in a lexical list were used in the related articles? If the list is good and the articles are well written, the correlation will be high. If the list is poor or the articles are badly written (with a lot of off-topic material), the correlation will be low. To what extent is semantic targeting a comment on the literary quality of a web page?

It also makes an interesting exercise to choose a topic with which you are unfamiliar, and note the greater level of difficulty in deciding which items on a web page are relevant and which are not. Is the difficulty more a function of your lack of linguistic (dictionary) knowledge or of your general (encyclopedic) knowledge?

Notes

1 LINGUISTIC PERSPECTIVES

1 http://www3.interscience.wiley.com/journal/117979306/home.
2 For the defining properties of human language, as opposed to other communication systems, see C.F. Hockett, *A course in modern linguistics* (New York: Macmillan, 1958) and the summary in D. Crystal, *The Cambridge encyclopedia of language* (Cambridge: Cambridge University Press, 3rd edition, 2010, chapter 64).
3 Including my own *Language and the Internet* (Cambridge: Cambridge University Press, 2001; 2nd edition, 2006).
4 http://www.languageatinternet.de/about.journal_html.
5 These arguments, and the sources of the statistics reported below, are given in full in D. Crystal, *Txtng: the gr8 db8* (Oxford: Oxford University Press, 2008).
6 For a brief account of semantics, see D. Crystal, *The Cambridge encyclopedia of language* (Cambridge: Cambridge University Press, 3rd edition, 2010, chapter 17); see also J. Lyons, *Semantics* (Cambridge: Cambridge University Press, 1977).
7 T. Berners-Lee, *Weaving the web* (London: Orion Business Books, 1999); the next quotation is from p. 203.

8 http://www.nielsen-online.com/pr/pr_071218_UK.pdf.

9 http://blog.twitter.com/2009/11/whats-happening.html.

10 For the notion of graphic translatability, see M. Twyman, The graphic presentation of language, *Information Design Journal* 3, 1982, pp. 1–22.

2 THE INTERNET AS A MEDIUM

1 See Chapter 1, note 2 above.

2 The following summary is based on the table and associated discussion in D. Crystal, *Language and the Internet* (Cambridge: Cambridge University Press, 2nd edition, 2006, p. 28).

3 D.F. Witmer and S.L. Katzman, Online smiles: does gender make a difference in the use of graphic accents? *Journal of Computer-Mediated Communication* 2(4), 1997. http://www.ascusc.org/jcmc/vol2/issue4/witmer1.html.

4 N. Baron, *Always on: language in an online and mobile world* (Oxford: Oxford University Press, 2008, p. 65).

5 T.Ö. Berglund, Disrupted turn adjacency and coherence maintenance in instant messaging conversations, *Language@Internet* 2009. http://www.languageatinternet.de/articles/2009/2106.

6 T. Berners-Lee, *Weaving the web* (London: Orion Business Books, 1999, p. 133).

7 U. Pfeil, P. Zaphiris, and C.S. Ang, Cultural differences in collaborative authoring in Wikipedia, *Journal of Computer-Mediated Communication* 12(1), 2006. http://jcmc.indiana.edu/vol12/issue1/pfeil.html.

8 http://www.webarchive.org.uk.

9 S. Herring, A faceted classification scheme for computer-mediated discourse, *Language@Internet* 2007. http://www.languageatinternet.de/articles/2007/761.

10 D. Crystal, *Language and the Internet* (Cambridge: Cambridge University Press, 2nd edition, 2006); *Txtng: the gr8 db8* (Oxford: Oxford University Press, 2008).

3 A MICROEXAMPLE: TWITTER

1 See for example C. Honeycutt and S.C. Herring, Beyond microblogging: conversation and collaboration via Twitter, in *Proceedings of*

42nd Hawaii International Conference on System Sciences, 2009. http://www.computer.org/portal/web/csdl/doi/10.1109/HICSS. 2009.602.

2 Emerging stylistic variation in retweeting is studied in D. Boyd, S. Golder, and G. Lotan, Tweet, tweet, retweet: conversational aspects of retweeting on Twitter, in *Proceedings of 43rd Hawaii International Conference on System Sciences*, 2010. http://www. danah.org/papers/TweetTweetRetweet.pdf.

3 For example: http://www.tutwow.com/tips/make-the-most-of-your-140-twitter-characters.

4 For the distinction between minor and major sentences, see D. Crystal, *Rediscover grammar* (London: Longman, 2004, chapter 2).

5 Two-thirds of the turns in instant messaging are six words or less: D. Crystal, *Language and the Internet* (Cambridge: Cambridge University Press, 2nd edition, 2006, p. 251).

6 http://www.pearanalytics.com/blog/2009/twitter-study-reveals-interesting-results-40-percent-pointless-babble.

7 For example, B. Krishnamurthy, P. Gill, and M. Arlitt, A few chirps about Twitter, in *Proceedings of 1st Workshop on Online Social Networks* (New York: ACM Press, 2008, pp. 19–24). http://www.cs.st-andrews.ac.uk/~tristan/sigcomm08/workshops/wosn/papers/p19.pdf; B. Huberman, D. Romero, and F. Wu, Social networks that matter: Twitter under the microscope, *First Monday* 14(1), 2009. http://firstmonday.org/htbin/cgiwrap/bin/ojs/index.php/fm/article/view/2317/2063.

8 http://www.prweb.com/releases/2009/04/prweb2367764.htm; http://royal.pingdom.com/2009/11/27/study-males-vs-females-in-social-networks; http://www.businessinsider.com/everything-you-need-to-know-about-whos-using-twitter-2010-4.

9 http://www.nytimes.com/2009/08/26/technology/internet/26twitter.html?_r=1; http://royal.pingdom.com/2010/02/16/study-ages-of-social-network-users.

10 The two surveys are: http://blogs.hbr.org/cs/2009/06/new_twitter_research_men_follo.html; http://themetricsystem.rjmetrics.com/2010/01/26/new-data-on-twitters-users-and-engagement.

11 N. Carr, Is Google making us stupid? *Atlantic Magazine* (July/August 2008). http://www.theatlantic.com/magazine/archive/2008/07/is-google-making-us-stupid/6868; also, *The Shallows* (Norton, 2010).

4 LANGUAGE CHANGE

1 S.I. Landau, On matters lexicographical: scientific and technical entries in American dictionaries, *American Speech* 49(3/4), 1974, pp. 241–4.

2 For a fuller account, see D. Crystal, *Language and the Internet* (Cambridge: Cambridge University Press, 2nd edition, 2006, chapter 3).

3 A list of such extensions (as of 2004) is given in D. Crystal, *A glossary of netspeak and textspeak* (Edinburgh: Edinburgh University Press, 2004).

4 R. Ling, An analysis of SMS use by a random sample of Norwegians, in R. Ling and P. Pedersen (eds), *Mobile communications: renegotiation of the social sphere* (London: Springer, 2005, pp. 335–49).

5 C. Waseleski, Gender and the use of exclamation points in computer-mediated communication: an analysis of exclamations posted to two electronic discussion lists, *Journal of Computer-Mediated Communication* 11(4), 2006. http://jcmc.indiana.edu/vol11/issue4/waseleski.html.

6 S. Greenbaum, Spelling variants in British English, *Journal of English Linguistics* 19, 1986, pp. 258–68.

7 H.P. Grice, Logic and conversation, in P. Cole and J.L. Morgan (eds), *Syntax and semantics 3: speech acts* (New York: Academic Press, 1975, pp. 41–58).

8 E. Adami, ELF and sign-making practices on YouTube: between globalization and specificities, in R. Facchinetti, D. Crystal, and B. Seidlhofer (eds), *From international to local English – and back again* (Bern: Peter Lang, 2010, pp. 235–64).

9 For example, T. Vestergaard and K. Schrøder, *The language of advertising* (Oxford: Blackwell, 1985); A. Bell, *The language of news media* (Oxford: Blackwell, 1991). See also D. Crystal and D. Davy, *Investigating English style* (London: Longman, 1969).

5 A MULTILINGUAL INTERNET

1 M. Specter, World, wide, web: 3 English words, *New York Times*, 14 April 1996.

2 United States Internet Council, Third annual survey of net trends: a release, 2001. http://www.usinternetcouncil.org.

3 Data in this paragraph from ITU World Telecommunication/ ICT Indicators, 2007; see http://www.itu.int/newsroom/features/ ict_africa.html.

4 See further, L.A. Grenoble and L.J. Whaley, *Saving languages: an introduction to language revitalization* (Cambridge: Cambridge University Press, 2006).

5 http://www.attitudeweb.be/doc/resources/studies/ebusiness_adoption_around_the_world.pdf.

6 There is an excellent review of the methodological issues in D. Pimienta, D. Prado, and Á. Blanco, *Twelve years of measuring linguistic diversity in the Internet: balance and perspectives* (Paris: UNESCO, 2009). http://unesdoc.unesco.org/images/0018/001870/187016e.pdf.

7 http://www.worldlanguage.com/; http://globalrecordings.net/languages.

8 http://portal.unesco.org/ci/en/ev.php-URL_ID=13475&URL_DO=DO_TOPIC&URL_SECTION=201.html.

9 http://sel.icann.org/meetings/.../transcript-board-meeting-30oct09-en.txt.

10 http://www.unicode.org/standard/supported.html; http://www.unicode.org/charts.

11 See, for example, D. Cunliffe and R. Harries, Promoting minority-language use in a bilingual online community, *New Review of Hypermedia and Multimedia* 11(2), 2005, pp. 157–80.

12 P. Gerrand, Estimating linguistic diversity on the Internet: a taxonomy to avoid pitfalls and paradoxes, *Journal of Computer-Mediated Communication* 12(4), 2007. http://jcmc.indiana.edu/vol12/issue4/gerrand.html. See also the report in note 6 above.

13 J.C. Paolillo and A. Das, *Evaluating language statistics: the ethnologue and beyond*. Report prepared for the UNESCO Institute for Statistics, 2006. http://ella.slis.indiana.edu/~paolillo/research/u_lg_rept.pdf.

14 UNESCO Portal, In focus: measures and indicators, 2006. http://portal.unesco.org/ci/en/ev.php-URL_ID=20973&URL_DO=DO_TOPIC&URL_SECTION=201.html.

15 Personal communication.

6 APPLIED INTERNET LINGUISTICS

1 The background is explained in D. Crystal, *Just a phrase I'm going through: my life in language* (Abingdon: Routledge, 2009, chapter

19). Much of this chapter reflects the projects developed for AND (Rotterdam), Crystal Reference Systems, and Adpepper Media. For two of the outcomes, see http://www.isense.net and http://www.site-screen.com.

2 D. Crystal, *A dictionary of linguistics and phonetics* (London: Blackwell, 6th edition, 2008).

3 http://www.dmoz.org.

4 For example, the procedure (Semantic NLP, i.e. Natural Language Processing) developed by Kathleen Dahlgren for Cognition: http://www.cognition.com/pdfs/Cognition_Semantic_NLP_for_Search_Overview.pdf.

5 See Chapter 4, note 6.

6 http://dublincore.org/.

7 A FORENSIC CASE STUDY

1 For example, in the UK the Child Exploitation and Online Protection Centre: http://www.ceop.gov.uk/; in the USA the National Center for Exploited and Missing Children: http://www.missingkids.com/missingkids/servlet/PageServlet?LanguageCountry=en_US&PageId=169.

2 For an algorithmic approach based on practices in natural language processing, see the Isis project: 'Protecting children in online social networks': http://www.comp.lancs.ac.uk/isis/.

3 R. O'Connell, A typology of child cyberexploitation and online grooming practices. Paper delivered to the Netsafe conference, Auckland, July 2003. Cyberspace Research Unit, University of Central Lancashire.

4 For this part of the investigation, I acknowledge the role of Martin Lee of Oxdigital, who provided the initiative for this study and wrote the software that was used to test it.

8 TOWARDS A THEORETICAL INTERNET LINGUISTICS

1 M. Twyman, The graphic presentation of language, *Information Design Journal* 3, 1982, pp. 1–22.

2 For MUDs, MOOs, and other innovations in virtual worlds, see D. Crystal, *Language and the Internet* (Cambridge: Cambridge University Press, 2nd edition, 2006, chapter 6).

3 http://news.bbc.co.uk/1/hi/magazine/8698174.stm.

4 B. Plester, C. Wood, and P. Joshi, Exploring the relationship between children's knowledge of text-message abbreviations and school literacy outcomes, *British Journal of Developmental Psychology* 27, 2009, pp. 145–61.

5 D. Crystal, *Txtng: the gr8 db8* (Oxford: Oxford University Press, 2008), where similarities across 11 languages are illustrated.

6 The original account is D. Sperber and D. Wilson, *Relevance: communication and cognition* (Oxford: Blackwell, 1986, 2nd edition, 1995). The quotation is from a paper, 'Relevance theory', at http://www. phon.ucl.ac.uk/home/PUB/WPL/02papers/wilson_sperber.pdf.

7 S. Lawrence and C. Lee Giles, Accessibility of information on the web, *Nature* 400, 1999, p. 107.

8 D. Crystal, *By hook or by crook* (London: HarperCollins, 2007, p. xi).

9 D. Crystal (ed.), *The new Penguin factfinder* (London: Penguin, 2003).

10 http://www.ace.mmu.ac.uk/eae/weather/Older/Depressions.html.

11 For netiquette guides, see D. Crystal, *Language and the Internet* (Cambridge: Cambridge University Press, 2nd edition, 2006, chapter 3).

9 RESEARCH DIRECTIONS AND ACTIVITIES

1 http://jcmc.indiana.edu; http://www3.interscience.wiley.com/journal/117979306/home?CRETRY=1&SRETRY=0; http://www.languageatinternet.de. See also the Association of Internet Researchers: http://aoir.org, and especially their list archives: http://listserv.aoir.org/pipermail/air-l-aoir.org/.

2 See the account at http://www.spinvox.com.

3 See the account at http://www.bury.com/us.

4 D. Crystal, *Txtng: the gr8 db8* (Oxford: Oxford University Press, 2008, p. 22).

5 http://twictionary.pbworks.com; http://twittonary.com.

6 http://unicode.org/charts/PDF/U2000.pdf.

7 For a summary of the main approaches to automatic translation, see D. Crystal, *The Cambridge encyclopedia of language* (Cambridge: Cambridge University Press, 3rd edition, 2010, chapter 57).

8 http://www.oclc.org/dewey/.

9 http://www.dmoz.org/.

10 http://www.google.com/support/merchants/bin/answer. py?hl=en&answer=160081.

FURTHER READING

Androutsopolous, J. (ed.) 2006. Sociolinguistics and computer-mediated communication. Special issue of *Journal of Sociolinguistics* 10(4).

Baron, N. 2008. *Always on: language in an online and mobile world*. Oxford: Oxford University Press.

Boardman, M. 2004. *The language of websites*. Abingdon: Routledge.

Crystal, D. 2006. *Language and the Internet*, 2nd edition. Cambridge: Cambridge University Press.

Crystal, D. 2008. *Txtng: the gr8 db8*. Oxford: Oxford University Press.

Danet, B. and Herring, S.C. (eds) 2007. *The multilingual Internet: language, culture, and communication online*. New York: Oxford University Press.

Deneke, L. 2007. *Computer-mediated communication*. Saarbrücken: VDM.

Myers, G. 2010. *The discourse of blogs and wikis*. London: Continuum.

Ooi, V.B.Y. 2009. Computer-mediated language and corpus linguistics, in Y. Kawaguchi, M. Minegishi, and J. Durand (eds), *Corpus analysis and variation in linguistics*. Amsterdam: John Benjamins, 103–20.

Posteguillo, S., Esteve, M.J., and Gea-Valor, M.L. 2007. *The texture of Internet: netlinguistics in progress*. Newcastle: Cambridge Scholars Publishing.

Spink, A. and Jansen, B.J. 2004. *Web search: public searching of the web*. Dordrecht: Kluwer.

Thurlow, C., Lengel, L., and Tomic, A. 2004. *Computer-mediated communication*. Newbury Park, CA: Sage.

INDEX